INTERSTELLAR

Photographer Mick Rock directed Bowie's promotional video for "Life on Mars?" backstage at London's Earls Court arena on May 12, 1973.

CONTENTS

ON THE COVER
David Bowie in front of the cover photo from his 1973 album *Aladdin Sane*, originally taken by Duffy. Photograph by Herb Ritts, 1989.

ON THE BACK COVER
Pin Ups photo session, August 1973. Photograph by Mick Rock.

DIAMOND DOG
At this 1974 photo shoot, the dog kept trying to bite the flash, said Terry O'Neill. "Every time it went off, he jumped. [Bowie] didn't turn a bloody hair— he was zonked out at the time, all the time. But he was such a class act."

REBEL REBEL

Throughout his life, DAVID BOWIE *fought the boring restrictions of everyday life. Yet as he slipped from one* PERSONA *to the next, it became less clear where he hoped that fight would take him. His* CRYPTIC FINAL WORKS *offer an answer, and help* UNLOCK THE MANY MYSTERIES *spread across his career.*

›PHOTOGRAPH *by* TERRY O'NEILL

ENDING UP

From his post-war London CHILDHOOD *to his debauched* SUPERSTARDOM
to his sublime EXPERIMENTAL *period, rock's greatest* SHAPE-SHIFTER *rarely stopped
running to catch a glimpse of what he was leaving behind.*

› **WORDS** *by* **MARC SPITZ**

SEEING RED
Bowie wears a zoot suit
during the *Diamond
Dogs* days of 1974, just
one of his myriad guises.

David Bowie was already thinking about the end as he sat in record producer Tom Ayres's home in the Hollywood Hills in February 1971. Every eye in the room was on him, and everything on the planet seemed different that night. Gene Vincent contributed another surreal moment to Bowie's new life. As a teenager, Bowie, then known as David Jones, had seen Vincent and his fearsome-looking Blue Caps on screen in the rock 'n' roll cavalcade *The Girl Can't Help It*. Vincent now walked with a limp, after a car accident, and seemed to Bowie a kind of rock 'n' roll Frankenstein. But there he was in Ayres's house in three dimensions, being introduced to the younger star. Bowie was traveling a path now, and would not be able to return. His career, which had heretofore been a series of crushing false starts (including a folky debut album that flopped in 1967), was maybe, just maybe, taking off.

When he had arrived in America days earlier, there were no celebrities and few stares to greet him. (After landing at Dulles, near D.C., he was detained at customs for questioning because of his unusual outfit.) Squired by Ron Oberman, his artist and repertoire rep from Mercury Records, Bowie later bedded down in a cold Holiday Inn in Times Square before making his way to the label's office in Chicago to gin up support for his new album, *The Man Who Sold the World*, his third. The only interest in him seemed to be regarding the provenance of the dress he wore on the U.K. version of the album cover, a silken, knee-length gown from London designer Mr. Fish. ("A man's dress," the singer insisted.) The U.S. release replaced that image with a tacky cartoon, so Bowie brought along a similar garment as a conversation piece. The music itself was Bowie's hardest rock since the early '60s.

Yes, *the early '60s.*

While only 24, this "new" artist was hardly green. He had been in the Konrads at Bromley Tech, his suburban high school. He was a former Manish Boy and member of the Lower Third when British blues was booming. He'd held tenure in the folk performance troupe Feathers, which became the short-lived Bowie and Hutch—a kind of poor man's Simon and Garfunkel—after his girlfriend Hermione Farthingale exited.

Not for lack of trying, and trying again, David Bowie had enjoyed exactly one semi-successful single, "Space Oddity," which arrived just days before the Apollo 11 moon landing in the summer of 1969. His subsequent second album, *David Bowie*, was a commercial failure. It was said the only reason Mercury kept him on the roster was that Bowie's wife and creative foil Angie had a friendship with executive Lou Reizner, who much preferred Rod Stewart, the label's other hopeful.

Bowie had suitors, mentors (including the eccentric dancer/mime Lindsay Kemp), and a manager, Kenneth Pitt, who seemed willing to exert all their energies on making him a star. Now Pitt was gone. Angie didn't think he was accomplishing much, for one, and her husband and personal cause had recently partnered with a new manager, a solicitor's clerk named Tony DeFries. Given to fur coats and cigars, the flamboyant DeFries wanted to ensure Bowie would be bigger than Elvis, with whom the singer shared a birthday.

Of course, none of this success had happened yet. But it seemed at least possible as Bowie sat there in Ayres's house, along with a cooing Rodney Bingenheimer (later an influential D.J.) and his towering partner in partying Kim Fowley (the controversial impresario who would later launch the Runaways). David Bowie was finally being noticed. Both Bingenheimer and Fowley had prized *The Man Who Sold the World*, produced for maximum intensity by the American Tony Visconti (who also played bass) and featuring intricate guitar work from a Hull native named Mick Ronson. Drummer Woody Woodmansey's presence made the combo a proto version of Bowie's most iconic backing band, the Spiders from Mars. Within a year or so, Visconti would relinquish the bassist position to the mutton-chopped Trevor Bolder and content himself with producing timeless albums for Bowie and others, including T. Rex (featuring Bowie's friend, Marc Bolan). It was all beginning to happen. But nobody at Ayres's knew, on that chilly night, just how far the

skinny kid with the damaged left eye—permanently blackened from a teenage punch—could see. All the way to the very end, perhaps.

According to Fowley, at one point, during what would become an endless series of parties over the next year leading up to Bowie-mania, Bowie cornered him and whispered, "How should I end up?"

Fowley, never at a loss for words, thought about it for a moment and said, "In a suit. Like Frank Sinatra."

In the last published photos of David Bowie, which were released shortly after he passed away at 69 on January 10, he's in that suit, a well-tailored black one, wearing a fedora—just like Sinatra (see page 13).

For a while at least, everything Tony DeFries promised David Bowie came true. He did return to America in 1972, an RCA signee with really good seats to Elvis's concert at Madison Square Garden. Members of Andy Warhol's Factory were put on the payroll of DeFries' company, MainMan, to make sure that word of Bowie's style and talent got around to the right people. *Hunky Dory*—the album Bowie wrote in Haddon Hall, a dilapidated mansion in leafy Beckenham, outside London, where he and Angie were busy raising their son Zowie—not only collected the sights and sounds of his humble American trip, but it would also cement Bowie's penchant for creating his future through song, then living it out. If he could not physically control a circumstance, he would steer it as best he could with his will and skills and Angie. And when even that didn't work, he would invent a character, like a novelist or playwright, and omnisciently control *that* poor soul's fate—producing and killing alter egos, creating at all times, never stopping, never slowing down until the end came. The quicker the alter ego bled into Bowie himself, the more certain he was to be doomed to the dustbin.

Where did this compulsion to know and control how something "ends up" come from? Armchair shrinks might cite World War II as an early source of this drive. Bowie's rough-and-tumble Brixton neighborhood was still damaged by German bombs when he grew up there. Every adult had a story about the war: impossible cruelty, death. Then there was madness. Bowie, while not clinically diagnosed, was pathologically shy, effortlessly odd, addicted to provocation. Schizophrenia lurked and sometimes lunged from his mother's side. His older half-brother, Terry Burns, was never able to live a life free of the disease. Terry had good years, bad years, horrifying episodes, periods of disappearance, each of which impacted the young David deeply. As a boy, David worshipped Terry, and most likely feared him too. Various other relatives, including an aunt, also reportedly fought the disease, and as Bowie became very famous, he might have known, given the proximity to schizophrenia, that it can be latent. As Bowie became very famous and his life more stressful and calamitous, it's possible that he feared he might one day simply wake up insane himself. Bowie's drugs of choice during these glitter years were speedy. He wasn't a junkie. Cocaine was his thing. And so we get quickness, the pivots, eluding the scary monsters and super creeps of his own genealogy. (Terry threw himself in front of a train in 1985.)

It's bad biographer form to psychoanalyze one's subject, and amateurish to read a subject's life in their lyrics, but it's hard to listen to Bowie's "All the Madmen," "Breaking Glass," "I'm Deranged," and "Jump They Say" without thinking of the writer's lifelong fixation with insanity. For someone who had it all and knew what it was like to have nothing, Bowie was one morbid guy. His fifth album, 1972's *The Rise and Fall of Ziggy Stardust and the Spiders From Mars*, the masterpiece that would confirm the suspicion that it was all happening, is not what one would call uplifting. In "Five Years," the news was out that "Earth was really dying." A half-decade, that's all we had. Even "All the Young Dudes" (the 1972 hit that Bowie wrote for Mott the Hoople), often assumed to be an anthem for young ravers, contains the lyric "Don't want to stay alive when you're 25." And who else would stop a stonking glitter-rock concert to bum out the entire venue with a version of Belgian crooner Jacques Brel's "My Death"? Who would dare? And why?

Many of Bowie's heroes (some introduced to him by Terry, including James Dean) did not have much time on Earth, but when a real artist is blessed with longevity, he or she *works*. And Bowie worked at an astounding rate: two full albums in 1973; another in 1974, including plans for an elaborate film based on the George Orwell novel *1984*; a theatrical concert tour also with Orwellian themes; an unpublished autobiography; drawings and paintings and models; production work and mentorship for both his own heroes, like Lou Reed and Iggy Pop, as well as a young Luther Vandross, a key player in Bowie's shift from glitter rock to plastic soul.

And what of those shifts? Were they, too, the almost reflexive decisions of a man on the run? David Bowie owes us no explanation any more than Picasso does for leaving Blue for Rose. An artist follows the inner voice and ventures ahead if that's where the body and the muse take him or her. If people get hurt along the way, it's really a case of the frog and the scorpion, isn't it? Kenneth Pitt might have been the first, but he certainly was not the last victim of Bowie's propensity toward head-spinning ▸ *continued on page 10*

1947

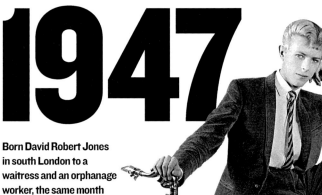

Born David Robert Jones in south London to a waitress and an orphanage worker, the same month and day as Elvis Presley.

1961
Father gives him first musical instrument for Christmas, a plastic saxophone.

1962
Joins first band, the Konrads, who play dances and parties.

1965 Changes
stage name from "Davie Jones" to "David Bowie" (after American frontiersman Jim Bowie).

1967 Enrolls in
the Covent Garden Dance Centre, learns how to mime; releases first album, the folky *David Bowie*.

1969

Scores first major hit with single "Space Oddity," which is played by the BBC during the Apollo II moon landing.

1970
Releases third album, *The Man Who Sold the World*, which many consider his first proper LP; marries Angela Barnett.

1971

Releases *Hunky Dory*, son Duncan
Zowie Haywood Jones is born.

1972

Releases *The Rise and Fall of Ziggy Stardust and the Spiders from Mars*; co-produces Lou Reed's *Transformer*.

PHOTOGRAPH BY SUKITA

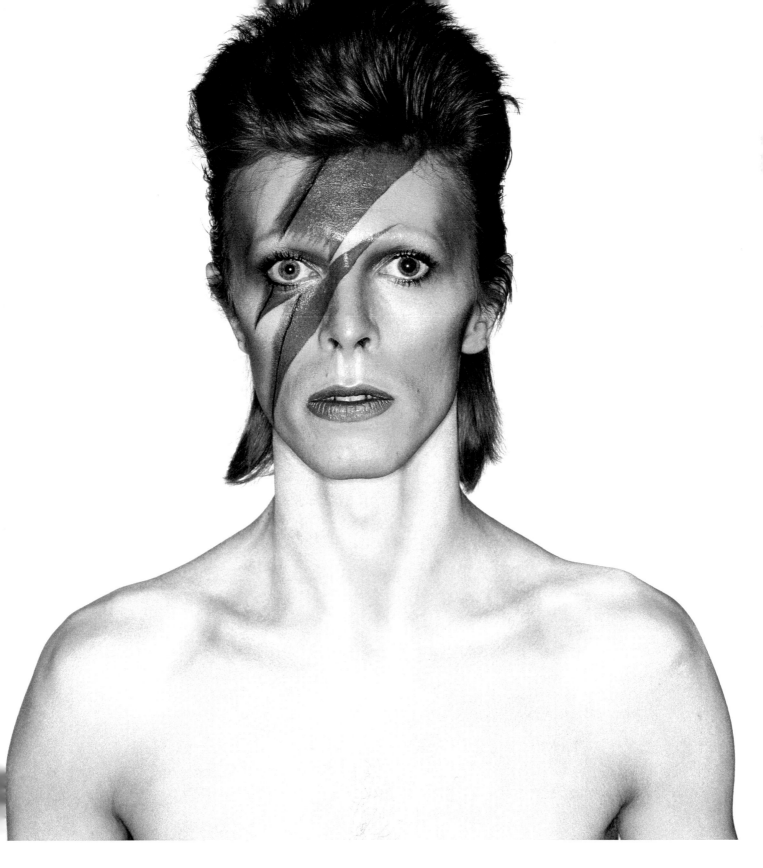

1973

Kills off Ziggy Stardust on final tour date, then resurrects him in TV performance *1980 Floor Show* later that year; *Aladdin Sane* debuts at No. 1 in the U.K., and reaches No. 17 in the U.S.; produces *People from Bad Homes* for girlfriend Ava Cherry, unreleased until 1995.

PHOTOGRAPH BY DUFFY

▸ *continued from page 6* ch-ch-ch-change. "Ha ha ha, hee hee hee, I'm the laughing gnome and you can't catch me," Bowie sang in what is often considered his worst song, 1967's "The Laughing Gnome." "Sometimes I feel the need to move on, and so I pack a bag and move on," he stated with a bit more dignity on his album *Lodger* a dozen years later. (By 1975, Tony DeFries would go the way of Kenneth Pitt, amid the inevitable legal clashes.)

On July 3, 1973, at the very height of their fame, Bowie announced his "retirement" on stage without warning his band (only Mick Ronson knew). Bowie would abort an enormously expensive *Diamond Dogs* tour midway through and re-invent it as a soul review. He had the money, the power, and the chutzpah to use whim as a paintbrush and not feel, or at least reveal, a shred of guilt over the wreckage. Hurt feelings, damaged careers, and, in the case of Angie, ruined marriages were quickly cleaned up by somebody else.

It went the other way too. People who had not heard from Bowie in decades would receive warm emails from him out of the blue. The man who supposedly hated nostalgia would modernize a favorite, often obscure, vintage tune, as he did on the unreleased album *Toy*, which leaked in 2011.

One of David Bowie's greatest talents was his ability to find stellar musicians to collaborate with (Carlos Alomar, Earl Slick, and Reeves Gabrels were, along with Ronson, among his most famous guitarists), but this didn't mean they were "in the band," even if they got used to the jet-setting lifestyle. Bowie was, as nearly all true artists are, alone at heart, no matter how many people were cheering or grabbing or demanding explanation or attention.

David Bowie survived punk when Lou Reizner's bet, Rod Stewart, got pilloried by it; he survived disco, too, and new wave. He even survived the David Bowie of the mid to late '80s. Not that his fallow years saw less manic creativity. Or darkness.

The rap on Bowie in the '80s was that he went mainstream with a new record deal and a slew of radio-ready, Nile Rodgers–produced songs: "Let's Dance," "China Girl," "Modern Love." The implication was that he sold out all the adoring misfits for a shot at MTV stardom. His saccharine 1987 album, *Never Let Me Down*, and pretentious Glass Spider tour seemed to erase in one summer a decade and a half of goodwill. But still, he survived: The movies he acted in during this peach-zoot-suited period—*The Hunger*; *Merry Christmas, Mr. Lawrence*; the telefilm *Baal*—were among the darkest of the era.

1974 *Diamond Dogs*, featuring "Rebel Rebel," is released, followed by an elaborate and expensive tour.

1975  Releases ninth studio album, *Young Americans*, featuring "Fame," his first No. I single in the U.S.

1976 Releases *Station to Station*, centering on Thin White Duke persona; stars in Nicolas Roeg sci-fi drama *The Man Who Fell to Earth*; expresses support for fascism and Adolf Hitler in interviews, opinions he later disavows.

1977 Releases *Low* and *"Heroes,"* the first two albums of his Berlin trilogy, made in collaboration with Brian Eno; parum-pum-pum-pums "Little Drummer Boy" with Bing Crosby on a Christmas TV special.

Death made its first move in 2004, and Bowie saw it coming. Many of his '70s contemporaries and collaborators were gone: Marc Bolan in a 1977 car wreck, John Lennon (who co-wrote and sang on "Fame") in a 1980 assassination. His 1999 album, '*hours...*,' was moody, mid-tempo, almost ghoulishly beautiful. Bowie had been recording *Heathen* on September 11, 2001.

And yet, as was his practice, Bowie seemed to be tripping up the Reaper. Until, that is, he was felled by a serious cardiac episode while touring in support of his 2003 album, *Reality*—a period, insiders say, when he sometimes felt chest pains but kept playing, kept moving, kept running. It finally placed him within reach of the horrible scythe.

After the *Reality* tour, he stayed inside. He moved, sometimes incognito, through New York City, where he'd been living since 1992. He chose his collaborators carefully: cameoing on Ricky Gervais' HBO comedy *Extras*, guesting with newly crowned indie-rock kings the Arcade Fire, voicing Lord Royal Highness on *SpongeBob SquarePants*. But mostly he was silent; enjoying, it was implied, domestic bliss with his longtime wife Iman and their daughter. (His son, who went back to his birth name, Duncan, is now a successful movie director.)

During this period, I wrote a fairly extensive book about Bowie, and when I went out to promote it, D.J.s and journalists asked me one question constantly: "Is he done?" I didn't say, but I had my theories. No. He is not. He cannot be done. An artist, a real one, doesn't just stop. Ingmar Bergman never retired. Did George Bernard Shaw? Is Woody Allen going to suddenly say, "O.K., finished"? Or Neil Young? Prince? I knew Bowie was doing... something.

On January 8, 2013, when *The Next Day* was announced and its first single was released without warning, I might have been one of the few who was not surprised. Bowie had taken to working in secret. The video for the second single, "The Stars (Are Out Tonight)," co-starring his distaff doppelgänger, actress Tilda Swinton, was funny, and in it he looked healthy. And with the April 2015 announcement of *Lazarus*, a musical Bowie co-created, based in part on the character he played in the 1976 Nicolas Roeg film *The Man Who Fell to Earth*, I thought, yes, he truly is activated. Even that oddball 10 years of silence, well, it almost felt like an art project in itself, a very, very long John Cage tribute. With *Lazarus*'s New York bow in December 2015, it was official: Ol' Blue and Black Eyes Was Back. He was doing it his way.

1979

Completes Berlin trilogy by releasing *Lodger*, performs in drag and as a puppet on *Saturday Night Live* with performance artists Klaus Nomi and Joey Arias.

1980 Releases

Scary Monsters (and Super Creeps); divorces Angela; stars in *The Elephant Man* on Broadway.

1981 Duets with

Freddie Mercury on Queen single "Under Pressure."

1983

Title track from *Let's Dance*, co-produced by Chic's Nile Rodgers, becomes his first U.S. No. 1 single since "Fame" in 1975.

1984 Releases

Tonight, featuring a duet with Tina Turner.

1985

Performs at London's Wembley Stadium for Live Aid to help raise money to fight the famine in Ethiopia; half-brother Terry Burns—who introduced Bowie to Tibetan Buddhism and Miles Davis, among other things—commits suicide.

There was something about *The Next Day* that gave me a chill, and it wasn't just the music. I never saw Death waiting in the corner. I don't see it in my own life and I did not see it in Bowie's, but the following year it became apparent to those who knew him well that He was there. And this time there was no sprint that could leave The Reaper behind. David Bowie had cancer, it was in his liver, and it was terminal.

I wonder if people realize how heroic it is to use your last few months on this Earth to create a play and release an album? I would imagine it's near impossible…unless, of course, you've been planning your exit for 45 years.

"How should I end up?"

When I think about *Blackstar*, I think about Kim Fowley and his reply to Bowie's question at a party. I don't turn my thoughts to the recording of the album, which again was done under a tarp of secrecy with a jazz combo and the loyal and ingenious Tony Visconti in tow. I think how I can't write an email if I have a headache or a hangnail.

But David Bowie for all his flaws, and there were many, was, as an artist at least, one of the Supermen. A *homo superior*. *Blackstar* is not just an album, it's the album people had been waiting for. The hook of *The*

Next Day was its shock existence, but *Blackstar* was art. Another birthday surprise, released January 8 at midnight, it would unfortunately presage an even bigger one.

Supposedly the play's cast and most of the crew did not know Bowie was ill, despite a decade of rumors. The director of *Blackstar*'s promotional videos, Johan Renck, had to be informed due to the singer's limited availability. The video for the song "Lazarus" finds Bowie in and out of bed, an afflicted old man, but also a maniac, dancing and grinning. "Look up here, I'm in heaven / I've got scars that can't be seen / I've got drama, can't be stolen / Everybody knows me now," a bedridden Bowie sings, with a sweep of gray hair and buttons affixed to bandages covering his eyes. The second Bowie, dressed in black, navigates a wardrobe. Does it contain a way out, another incarnation, or a Japanese frock, or is it, finally, a coffin?

One minute on January 9 "Lazarus" is just a really cool David Bowie video. The next, it's death as art. The man who never stopped creating had to literally be stopped by his own body. The Reaper, awaiting like He did in that bummer of a Jacques Brel song. Bowie's death didn't break the Internet so much as annex it. Included among the thousands of Facebook

1987 Releases disappointing *Never Let Me Down*; later admits, "You can tell I was terribly unhappy in the late '80s."

1989

Forms hard-rock band Tin Machine with ex–Iggy Pop band members Hunt and Tony Sales and guitarist Reeves Gabrels.

1992

Marries Somali model Iman in Florence in ceremony attended by Bono, Yoko Ono, and Brian Eno.

1995

Releases concept album, *Outside*, about a murderer; tours with Nine Inch Nails.

1996 Appears as Andy Warhol in biopic *Basquiat*; inducted into Rock & Roll Hall of Fame.

1997 Raises $55 million by issuing Bowie Bonds, promising a share of future royalties from his back catalog; releases *Earthling*.

1999 Releases *'hours...'*, featuring songs composed for the videogame Omikron: The Nomad Soul.

2000

Daughter Alexandria Zahra Jones is born.

2002 Releases 25th studio album, *Heathen*, widely considered his U.S. comeback.

posts were analyses of the new album, the new play, the new video, and his entire career—which has always lent itself to parsing and even encouraged occultists and conspiracy theorists.

Blackstar gave Bowie his first No. 1 album in the U.S. When someone dies, even someone really famous, it's been customary to mourn him for a day or so and then talk about television again. But Bowie's spirit seems to have entered the social networks like a ghost in the machine. "Thank you, everybody, for keeping Bowie alive a little longer on FB," someone posted. "Which David Bowie are you?" another asked. There were more memes and celebrity sendoffs and photos of flowers than can be calculated. Tickets for *Lazarus* were being scalped for four figures, and more people were listening, really listening, to a David Bowie record since back when he called Liz Taylor a good friend in 1976.

The enduring image of Sinatra, which Bowie absorbed as his own, is a heartbroken one: Frank after hours, post–last call, hat tilted, overcoat drooping in his hand. He's not the ring-a-dinging Rat Pack leader, he's alone at ebb tide. Bowie and Sinatra reportedly struck up a friendship in 1975, when both were recording at Cherokee Studios in Los Angeles (a paranoid Bowie creating *Station to Station* while having his swimming pool exorcised). Perhaps they discussed the burden of being the one in the room everyone looks at and still feeling, in his heart, that Death was right there, staring. Waiting. Or maybe, during one of those meetings in the studio, the Chairman took aside the Duke—who, by that point, had been experiencing chemically induced madness—and whispered, "Swing, baby, you're platinum."

Decades later, when Bowie donned his own black, sleekly cut, Sinatra-like suit and fedora for his final photo shoot, he seemed almost like Frank's opposite, on the streets in afternoon sun, light on his feet, his face cracking open with uncontainable laughter—suggesting, perhaps, that the emphasis of his question all those years ago hadn't been on the "end," but on the "up." How could he "end *up*"?

It appeared, as he looked straight into the camera, that he'd answered his own question and that it was the right way to go. □

Marc Spitz is the author of the best-selling Bowie: A Biography (Crown Archetype).

2013

Releases *The Next Day*, a spiritual follow-up to *"Heroes"*.

2003 Declines knighthood offered by Queen Elizabeth II: "It's not what I spent my life working for."

2005 Performs with Arcade Fire at Fashion Rocks benefit concert after touting band as one of his new favorites.

2015

Debuts off-Broadway play *Lazarus*.

2004 Stops concert in Prague early complaining of shoulder pain; days later, has emergency heart surgery for a blocked artery.

2006 Appears as Nikola Tesla in Christopher Nolan's *The Prestige*, about magicians in 19th-century London; sings "Changes" with Alicia Keys at a charity gig in New York, his final live performance.

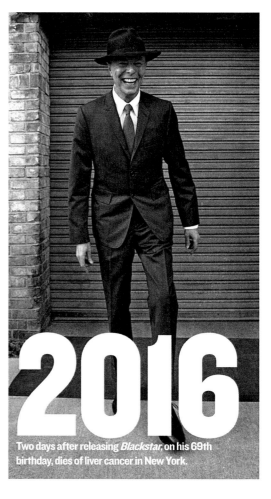

2016

Two days after releasing *Blackstar*, on his 69th birthday, dies of liver cancer in New York.

The Next Day

LAZARUS

MAN IN THE MIRROR
Mick Rock (who took this shot at Haddon Hall, Beckenham, U.K., in March 1972) has said, "For me, that's being an artist. You don't keep repeating yourself in the way you approach your creativity, and David, above all, did not."

STARMAN

While so many others lose their true selves in FAME, *Bowie seemed to* DISCOVER HIMSELF *in his celebrity and the spaced-out guises that helped him reach it, becoming a* LUMINARY *who made everyone around him burn* BRIGHTER.

›PHOTOGRAPH *by* MICK ROCK

There's a starman waiting in the sky / He'd like to come and meet us / But he thinks he'd blow our minds

REBEL NIGHTS

The New York rock scene of the '70s was
AN AMPED-UP, *sequin-studded, punk-powered* EXPLOSION
OF CREATIVITY. *Guess who fit right in.*

› **WORDS** *by* **LISA ROBINSON**
EXCERPTED FROM A PIECE ORIGINALLY PUBLISHED IN *VANITY FAIR*, NOVEMBER 2002
› **PHOTOGRAPH** *by* **MICK ROCK**

Some say the 1970s New York rock scene started in the 1960s with the Velvet Underground. Others insist that it began around 1968 with the Stooges and MC5 in Ann Arbor, Michigan. Or with Lou Reed's reconfigured Velvet Underground at Max's Kansas City in 1970. Or Patti Smith's poetry reading with Lenny Kaye on guitar at St. Mark's Church in February 1971. Or in London in 1970, when David Bowie began sewing those pre–Ziggy Stardust costumes.

The truth is that the truth is not so simple. What really happened is that several things happened, all at once, all over the world.

I remember I was knocked out by the [New York] Dolls. My first impressions were that they were the early Stones in strippers' clothes. Fabulous early R&B sound, but much sloppier and more vital. It was the humor, the fun and drunk "don't give a shit" attitude of the band, that was intoxicating.

—David Bowie, August 2002

On February 22, 1970, at the Roundhouse in London, David Bowie performed with his band Hype, in what he believes was the first British "glam rock" performance. "We had superhero costumes made," he says, "and I wore makeup and glitter for the first time."

In November 1971, with much fanfare, San Francisco drag-queen troupe the Cockettes came to New York for their opening of *Tinsel Tarts in a Hot Coma* at the East Village's Anderson Theater. In the audience that night were the Ahmet Erteguns, Rex Reed, Gore Vidal with Angela Lansbury, Elaine Kaufman, and Diana Vreeland. Fran Lebowitz was an usher. From then on, whenever a rhinestone or a sequin turned up in rock and roll, you could make a case for tracing it back to the Cockettes. Or to the Theater of the Ridiculous,

where John Vaccaro directed Warhol "superstar" Jackie Curtis and actress Penny Arcade in the low-camp *Heaven Grand in Amber Orbit*. Or to *Pork*, the 1971 show based on tapes of Brigid Polk's phone conversations with Andy Warhol, directed by Tony Ingrassia and starring actor Tony Zanetta, drag rocker Wayne County, and, most important, platinum-blonde Cyrinda Foxe. (The only female Marilyn Monroe look-alike in this scene, Foxe was David Johansen's girlfriend, Bowie's introduction to the New York Dolls, the "trois" in the alleged Bowie ménage, the inspiration for Bowie's song "Jean Genie," an apparent role model for her contemporaries Angela Bowie and Debbie Harry, and, eventually, Aerosmith singer Steven Tyler's wife.) *Pork* went to London in August 1971, and an enthusiastic Bowie—who had already been working on his Ziggy Stardust show and costumes with designer Freddie Buretti—showed up, befriended the cast, and would later be accused of "borrowing" their style.

But, according to Bowie: "Many of my influences were primarily [British mime] Lindsay Kemp and his coterie. They were a much smaller and less-profiled Soho London outfit than the Warhol crowd, but nevertheless a highly flamboyant bunch who opened my eyes from 1967 on. As much as I enjoyed the Warhol crowd (temporarily) thematically, my map was already drawn."

This isn't a woman's dress, this is a man's dress.
—Iggy Pop, circa 1971

September 1971: I met David Bowie for the first time in the RCA Records New York offices. He had long hair, a floppy hat, and Mary Jane shoes. He didn't wear the dress he was photographed in when [Mercury Records rep] Rodney Bingenheimer took him around on the previous Valentine's Day, but the effect was the same.

RCA had just signed Bowie, Lou Reed, and the Kinks, and my husband, Richard, was a producer at the label. Bowie was with his manager, Tony

WALK ON THE WILD SIDE
In summer 1972, Bowie cozies up to Lou Reed; he would later perform with Reed at the former Velvet Underground singer's 50th birthday concert in 1997.

DeFries—who was straight out of the sleazy school of the British music business—and Bowie's artfully butch, boisterous wife, Angela. I started to tell him all about how he should meet the Warhol crowd, and then, as if on cue, in the door came Tony Zanetta, actress-poet-groupie Cherry Vanilla, and *Pork* stage manager Leee Black Childers—all of whom, it appeared, had already signed up to be part of DeFries' MainMan management company "staff." I arranged a small dinner that night at the Ginger Man restaurant near Lincoln Center. Despite the stories that have grown around this "fateful" meeting, it was relatively sedate. White tablecloths and filets mignons. Lou Reed, none too gregarious, was with his then wife, Bettye Kronstad (who I think later changed her name to Krista Kronstad). We called Danny Fields mid-meal to tell him to send Iggy up. We met Iggy later at Max's, and while no one remembers much about the evening, I do remember that Iggy was not stoned (that night), as the fiction in the movie *Velvet Goldmine* had it, and that he and Bowie instantly hit it off. The next day Iggy moved into the Warwick Hotel, where the MainMan camp was in residence. A few nights later, the Bowies, the Reeds, and DeFries came to our apartment. Three things stand out in my memory of the evening: Bettye/Krista go-go danced alone in the living room. A rare copy of the *East Village Other* with an article on the Velvet Underground disappeared. And Lou and David locked themselves in a small back room while Angela Bowie banged on the door, screeching for them to let her in.

December 1972: Lou Reed, Richard [Robinson], and I went to London, where Richard was producing Lou's first solo album. We were invited to a party at Bowie's house. David greeted us at the door flaunting

FRIENDS INDEED
With Mercury Records rep and scenester Rodney Bingenheimer; Iggy Pop, who would become Bowie's collaborator in Berlin, relaxes (below).

his new look—black-and-gray jumpsuit, red patent-leather boots, short, spiky orange hair. I burst out laughing. So, you've gone from *2001* to *A Clockwork Orange*. He laughed that wicked cackle with a full display of his [then] rotting teeth. Despite having been asked not to have liquor around, since Lou was not at his most delightful when bored and drunk [and he seemed very bored during the London sojourn], David teasingly dangled a bottle of Dewar's in front of us. Angela was in the kitchen cooking. Later that night the Bowies, their friends, Lou, Richard, and I all went to the gay dance club El Sombrero. When I left several hours later, Lou and David were on the dance floor, slow dancing.

To create an art movement, you have to set something up and then destroy it. The only thing to do is what the Dadaists, the Surrealists, did—complete amateurs who are as pretentious as hell—and just fuck it up the ass. Cause as much bad, ill feeling as possible. . . . You'll only create a movement when you have a rebellious cause.
—David Bowie, 1976

In July 1972, David Bowie invited a group of American journalists to see him perform the Ziggy Stardust and the Spiders from Mars show in Aylesbury, outside London. Playing that same weekend on another bill were the early punk sensations the Flamin' Groovies and the Stooges, and, at the King's Cross Cinema, Lou Reed. The famous Mick Rock photo of David, Lou, and Iggy was taken at an afternoon press conference at the Dorchester hotel; MainMan was now handling all three stars. Onstage, Lou wore black lipstick and was, as Lenny Kaye said tactfully, "not in the best shape." But later that year Bowie would produce Lou's *Transformer* and help Lou get his biggest hit—"Walk on the Wild Side"—and would then go on to produce two of Iggy's best albums: *The Idiot* and *Lust for Life*.

December 1974: I cannot believe what I saw on TV last night. David Bowie was on Dick Cavett's show as a special guest. Cavett came on minus a tie for this "hip" occasion and introduced Bowie as an artist who "changes

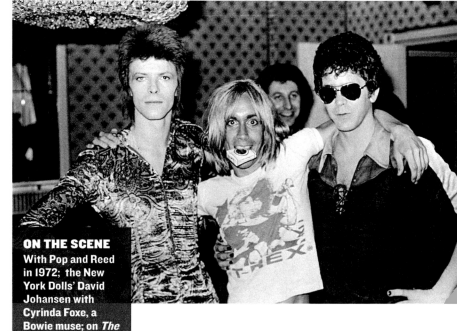

ON THE SCENE
With Pop and Reed in 1972; the New York Dolls' David Johansen with Cyrinda Foxe, a Bowie muse; on *The Dick Cavett Show* in 1974 (bottom).

like a chameleon." The audience cheered. Bowie performed (and I use this word loosely) "1984" and "Young Americans." Then he and Cavett sat down for a chat. David Bowie is obviously not a well man. He is thin beyond belief. Eyes flashing, fingers flickering, constantly tapping a cane—an absurd prop, but then again, perhaps he needs it. Cavett did not help matters much. In between almost constant sniffling, Bowie managed to get out that he isn't very academic, he reads only the good reviews, he likes working with a band. "How do you say your wife's name?" asked Cavett, grasping at straws. "I've seen it printed Angels and Angela. Which is the typo?" Huh? "Um, Angela. Angie," said David, who proceeded to talk about how she was an intellectual, a revelation to those of us who know Angela Bowie.

In 1973 the symbiosis that had marked Bowie's relationship with Lou Reed extended to Iggy, who was financially supported by MainMan. Holed up in the Hollywood Hills, Iggy dyed his hair platinum and took heroin almost full-time. "You know," he would say several years later, "when I met you and a lot of people in New York, well. . .you know where I come from [a trailer park outside Ann Arbor, Michigan], and I was thrown into a scene that was very. . .mondo. And I think it turned me a little bit evil."

Bowie didn't have an influence on me other than friendship. Friendship is a very underrated influence in these modern times. Basically, David and I exchanged information. It's great to meet somebody else who thinks they're always right.
—Iggy Pop, 1986 □

This piece appears in a slightly different form in Lisa Robinson's memoir, There Goes Gravity: A Life in Rock and Roll (Riverhead).

"THE AUDIENCE IS STILL THE ONLY THING THAT I CARE ABOUT, BECAUSE THEY WERE ALWAYS WITH ME."

TASTY LICKS
Taking a bite out of
Mick Ronson's guitar in
London in 1973.

**PHOTOGRAPH BY
ILPO MUSTO**

ANTHEMS FOR THE MOON

Unpacking the SCIENCE-FICTION *literature, movies, and TV shows that inspired Bowie's* SPACE ODYSSEY *and gave rise to* MAJOR TOM *and* ZIGGY STARDUST.

›**WORDS** *by* **JASON HELLER**
ORIGINALLY PUBLISHED ON PITCHFORK.COM, JANUARY 13, 2016
›**PHOTOGRAPH** *by* **DAVID BEBBINGTON**

The book's cover must have grabbed the young David Robert Jones. Illustrated in lurid yellow and green, it depicts a man and woman entering a shadowy forest. Behind them, a spaceship shaped like a giant light bulb perches on the surface of some strange planet. In the sky above, alien octopi bob like sentient balloons, peering down at the humans with a mix of curiosity and hunger. Written by science-fiction legend Robert A. Heinlein, *Starman Jones* was published in 1953, when Jones was 6 years old. The lad who would grow up to become David Bowie considered it a favorite. Surely he was captivated by the fact that the story's astronautical hero shared his last name—and that, with a bit of imagination, he might someday become his own kind of Starman Jones.

He never lost that fascination. The voraciously bookish Bowie absorbed not only Heinlein, but the works of such luminaries as Ray Bradbury and George Orwell, whose classics *The Illustrated Man* and *1984* would prove to be vital influences as he became popular music's ethereal, mercurial ambassador to science fiction. In the summer of 1969, the 22-year-old aspiring rock musician released "Space Oddity," the song that launched him into orbit. Like Bowie himself, the single's astronaut protagonist—Major Tom—was destined, or perhaps doomed, never to return to Earth.

The late '60s was a heady time for science, sci-fi, and music. The Apollo 11 mission culminated in a landing on the moon on July 20, 1969, marking a turn away from the vision of hippie utopianism, the back-to-basics movement that elevated pastoral romanticism over the hard logic of encroaching technocracy. As sociologist Philip H. Ennis noted, "It is probably not [an] hyperbole to assert that the Age of Aquarius ended when man walked on the moon. Not only was the countercultural infatuation with astrology given

ALL THAT GLITTERS

In London in September 1969, just a few months after the release of "Space Oddity."

HOLST THE PLANETS

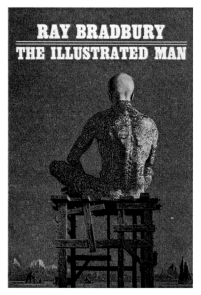

RAY BRADBURY
THE ILLUSTRATED MAN

new worlds

NUMBER 199
3s 6d

DOES SEX
HAVE A
FUTURE?

PLUS
LOVE POEMS
by C.M. Thomas

SPECULATIVE
FICTION

MUSIC &
BAD BOOKS

by the author of the #1 bestseller
BREAKFAST OF CHAMPIONS
**Kurt
Vonnegut,
jr.
Slaughter-
House
Five**

GALAXY QUEST
Above and right:
music, books, and
magazines that informed
Bowie's creations;
astronaut Chris Hadfield
strums "Space Oddity"
aboard the International
Space Station
in 2013 (far right).

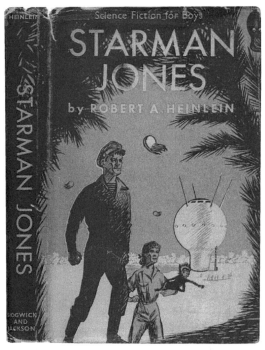

Science Fiction for Boys
STARMAN JONES
by ROBERT A. HEINLEIN
SIDGWICK AND JACKSON

a strong, television-validated antidote of applied astronomy, but millions of kids who had not signed up for either belief system were totally convinced."

Meanwhile, science fiction was making a different yet similarly seismic shift of its own. In 1964, a young editor named Michael Moorcock took the reins of *New Worlds*, a venerable British magazine that he used as a platform for avant-garde science fiction and fantasy. By 1969, *New Worlds* had become a beacon for transgressive work, publishing forward-thinking authors from both sides of the Atlantic such as J.G. Ballard, Samuel R. Delany, Thomas M. Disch, Brian Aldiss, Roger Zelazny, and Rachel Pollack (under the name Richard A. Pollack).

All these *New Worlds* authors, and many others like them, challenged the predominantly optimistic outlook and linear storytelling techniques of science fiction up to that point. Theirs were not simplistic tales of intrepid explorers such as Heinlein's *Starman Jones*. In their place, *New Worlds* substituted moral ambiguity, sexual fluidity, narrative experimentation, broken taboos, and sometimes even outright nihilism; Moorcock and crew wholeheartedly embraced William S. Burroughs's incursions into genre-twisting radicalism as an integral part of the sci-fi canon—and the genre's future.

Moorcock published some of his own work in *New Worlds*, and it exemplified his ideal: a style that became known as the New Wave. In particular, his Jerry Cornelius series of novels and short stories—1968's *The Final Programme* being the first book-length installment—summed up that wildly transitional period. In them, Cornelius is a mysterious, androgynous secret agent with a knack for sartorial elegance and introverted remove—and in his spare time, he's a rock star.

The parallels between Cornelius's chameleon-like existence and Bowie's are unmistakable. Both are products of swinging London's mod scene of the mid-'60s, where Bowie cut his teeth as an up-and-coming performer. In his scattershot quest for recognition, Bowie often switched up his stage names and identities, a process that eventually culminated in his androgynous image at the height of the glam movement in the early '70s, when he reinvented himself as Ziggy Stardust.

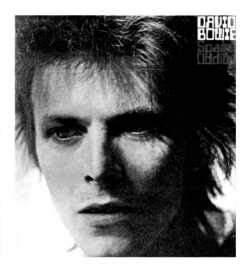

In its celebration of androgyny, glam lined up with Ursula K. Le Guin's visionary 1969 novel *The Left Hand of Darkness*, which takes place on an alien planet where transitions between genders are as routine as any other biological process. "Androgynous sexuality and extraterrestrial origin seemed to have provided two different points of identification for Bowie fans," notes Philip Auslander in *Performing Glam Rock: Gender and Theatricality in Popular Music*. "Whereas some were taken with his wo-manliness, others were struck by his spaciness."

During the formative years of the mid-'60s, Bowie was the frontman of a short-lived group named the Lower Third. And that rock band incorporated an odd choice of song into their repertoire: "Mars, the Bringer of War," a movement from *The Planets*, the orchestral suite by the English composer Gustav Holst. The suite was known to Bowie's generation primarily from its use as the theme to the popular *Quatermass* science-fiction serials produced by the BBC in the '50s. Bowie was a huge fan of *Quatermass*, once admitting that as a boy he would watch it "from behind the sofa when my parents thought I had gone to bed. After each episode I would tiptoe back to my bedroom rigid with fear, so powerful did the action seem to me." That power took a very firm hold of the young man's imagination; the theme of astronauts lost in space was the premise behind the first *Quatermass* serial, 1953's *The Quatermass Experiment*.

As the amphetamine-fueled mod scene morphed into the acid-fueled psychedelic scene, London became the laboratory in which Bowie began conducting experiments of his own—ones that sought to transmute science fiction and fantasy into the sounds of popular music.

Like most of his pre–"Space Oddity" output, Bowie's 1967 song "Karma Man" depicts a tattooed man whose elaborate body art tells wondrous and hideous tales. "It's pictured on the arms of the Karma Man," goes the refrain, a blatant reference to Bradbury's 1951 book *The Illustrated Man*, a collection of short stories framed by one of fantasy's ▶ *continued on page 104*

OTHER WORLDS
Clockwise from top left: the "Ashes to Ashes" video; a novel that features a character very similar to the singer; an alternate cover of Bowie's second album; Malcolm McDowell in *A Clockwork Orange*; Keir Dullea in *2001: A Space Odyssey*.

IGGY

In April 1976, Bowie traveled to Moscow with Iggy Pop, though his music had been banned there during the Soviet era.

FRIENDS LIKE THESE

A list of Bowie's ACQUAINTANCES *and* COLLABORATORS *would read like a who's who of 20th-century popular culture. What follows are a few snapshots from a lifetime filled with* CREATIVE CONNECTIONS.

TINA

Tina Turner duetted with Bowie on the title track of his 1984 album, *Tonight*; a live version of the song appeared on *Tina Live in Europe*.

MARC

Bowie performs with T. Rex frontman Marc Bolan on the final episode of Bolan's U.K. television show on September 7, 1977; the host died in a car accident nine days later.

LOU

Bowie and Lou Reed pucker up in front of Mick Jagger in 1973.

JOHN

The dapper Thin White Duke attends the Grammys in New York with John Lennon on March I, 1975; Bowie received a Lifetime Achievement Award in 2006.

BRYAN

With fellow glam-rock dandy Roxy Music frontman Bryan Ferry in Philadelphia in 1979.

MICK

The Rolling Stones singer Mick Jagger (with Bowie in London in 1987) recently said: "We had a lot in common in wanting to do big things onstage—using interesting designs, narratives, personalities."

MICK

A member of the Spiders from Mars, guitarist Mick Ronson (with Bowie in 1973) played on six of Bowie's studio albums.

WILLIAM

Bowie met one of his idols, William S. Burroughs, in 1973, when the author of such outré novels as *Naked Lunch* and *Junkie* interviewed him for *Rolling Stone*.

"THE FUTURE [IS] VERY IMPORTANT. DON'T WAIT FOR IT. WE MAKE THE FUTURE AS WE MAKE THE TRUTH."

THE EYES HAVE IT

"I looked at him as more an actor than a singer," Terry O'Neill has said. "Once he finished performing, he dropped the image and went back to being himself."

PHOTOGRAPH BY TERRY O'NEILL

FEELING PECKISH
Despite being seen with a typewriter in 1975, Bowie was known to employ the cut-up technique when writing lyrics: "I'm always amazed that people take what I say seriously. I don't even take what I *am* seriously."

BEAUTIFUL NONSENSE

In the lyrics to BLACKSTAR, *Bowie once again showcased his* ZEAL *in embracing the* ABSURD.

› **WORDS** *by* **BEN GREENMAN**

ORIGINALLY PUBLISHED ON THENEWYORKER.COM, JANUARY 9, 2016

› **PHOTOGRAPH** *by* **STEVE SCHAPIRO**

David Bowie's *Blackstar* is his second album since he resurfaced from what seemed like semi-retirement. As it turned out, it was a period of rejuvenation. *The Next Day*, released early in 2013, was a muscular rock record filled with snarling anthems and reflective ballads, and it acknowledged its connection to (or hostility toward) the past with its cover art, which featured an obscured image of the cover art of Bowie's 1977 album *"Heroes." Blackstar* is a different creature entirely. Rather than assembling a crack team of rock vets (and Bowie vets), *Blackstar* employs a new band anchored by New York jazz players like the pianist Jason Lindner and the saxophonist Donny McCaslin. The presence of jazz players has led to a mistaken characterization of *Blackstar* as a jazz record, which it isn't. It's a singer-songwriter record that is willing to stretch its compositions around instrumentation that's not typically associated with rock 'n' roll. It's also prime Bowie in its willingness to embrace nonsense.

From the beginning, Bowie showed an interest in exploring the fragmentation of identity and meaning. His career depended heavily on performance, which allowed him to actively deploy various signifiers inside and alongside his music—signifiers of gender, of sexual orientation, even of humanity itself. (The question of radical others, up to and including aliens, surface frequently in his early work.) At some point, he began to look more rigorously into the idea of meaninglessness, and to write songs that were willful participants in their own fragmentation. The most famous early example of this, of course, is the *Diamond Dogs* album, in which Bowie employed the cut-up method developed by William Burroughs and Brion Gysin. Scissors were taken to a text. Slips of paper were drawn at random. The results, subject to chance, were then fashioned into lyrics like these:

Meet his little hussy with his ghost-town approach
Her face is sans feature, but she wears a Dali brooch
Sweetly reminiscent, something mother used to bake
Wrecked up and paralyzed, Diamond Dogs are sable-ized

It was rare for Bowie to embrace clear meaning. The title of one of his most plainspoken songs, " 'Heroes,' " is suspended in a second set of quotation marks, largely to disrupt any straightforward interpretation. "Where Are We Now?," Bowie's beautifully fragile comeback ballad and the first single from *The Next Day*, was a conspicuous exception—it was a snapshot, relatively easy to parse, of an older man revisiting Berlin and wondering about the city's ch-ch-changes. But on much of the rest of the album he was as slippery as ever, and the same is true of *Blackstar*. The new album's title track and lead single opens with a ghostly, vaguely Middle Eastern chant.

In the villa of Ormen, in the villa of Ormen
Stands a solitary candle, ah-ah, ah-ah
In the center of it all, in the center of it all
Your eyes

On the day of execution, on the day of execution
Only women kneel and smile, ah-ah, ah-ah
At the center of it all, at the center of it all
Your eyes, your eyes

People said it was about ISIS, and then Bowie denied it. It's good that he denied it, because his songs should be about nothing, which in turn allows them to be about everything. In another song, "Girl Loves Me," Bowie latches onto a rubbery melody and the echoed, repeated refrain: "Where the fuck did Monday go?" It's evocative, but unexplained. Adding to the song's sense of obfuscation and evasion is the fact that many of the lyrics are in Nadsat, the language Anthony Burgess invented for his teen hooligans in *A Clockwork Orange*. There's also some Polari thrown in for good measure.

Cheena so sound, so titi up this malchick, say
Party up moodge, nanti vellocet round on
Tuesday
Real bad dizzy snatch makin' all the omeys
mad, Thursday
Popo blind to the polly in the hole by Friday

The way in which the lyrics thwart straightforward interpretation gives them power and a compelling sense of erotic menace. The British writer and intellectual historian Peter Watson has made a career of publishing books that set out to comprehensively summarize the field of human thought: most notably with *Ideas*, in 2005. His books are filled with reductions and lacunae, as any book purporting to summarize human thought must be. But they are also useful for picking out kernels. In *The Modern Mind*, in 2001, Watson gives an account of the growth of Surrealism in art, identifying the movement not only as a form of exploration but as a site of resistance:

> *But above all, taking their lead from dreams and the unconscious, their work showed a deliberate rejection of reason. Their art sought to show that progress, if it were possible, was never a straight line, that nothing was predictable, and that the alternative to the banalities of the acquisitive society, now that religion was failing, was a new form of enchantment.*

Rock 'n' roll started as a form of enchantment and has become, in large part, another symptom of the banality of our acquisitive society. By persisting in deliberately rejecting reason, Bowie reminds us that there are plenty of reasons to do so. The most naked moment on the new record is its final song, "I Can't Give Everything Away," which almost reads like a defense of a career of obscurantism.

> *I know something's very wrong*
> *The pulse returns for the prodigal sons*
> *The blackout hearts with flowered news*
> *With skull designs upon my shoes*
>
> *I can't give everything*
> *I can't give everything*
> *Away*

Seeing more and feeling less
Saying no but meaning yes
This is all I ever meant
That's the message that I sent

I can't give everything
I can't give everything
Away

Unless, of course, that isn't what it means at all.

Postscript: David Bowie's death is sad and surprising, though maybe just partly surprising. There were many rumors of illness even before the release of *The Next Day*, but the vitality of that record beat them back a bit. In the videos for *Blackstar*, Bowie looks frail, but he often looked frail. The news of his cancer and its advance seems to have been kept close. People will now look for hints in his recent music, and they'll find them. *The Next Day* is filled with a sense of loneliness and the struggle to connect, and *Blackstar* has several songs that seem to bridge life and death. "Lazarus," the song that everyone wants to see as a literal handling of the matter, was written for an Off Broadway play. That doesn't mean that the song is not a way of facing into death, but it also doesn't mean that it is. For me the album's contribution to the vexing question of human existence lies in the way in which Bowie struggles to articulate the human struggle to articulate. That seemed true even before Bowie's death, and it seems truer now. It brings to mind Samuel Beckett's last poem, "What Is the Word," which Beckett wrote in bed in a nursing home, in Paris, the year before his death. Except that he didn't really write it at all: It's a translation of an earlier work, "Comment Dire," that he wrote in French in 1982. The inexpressible is expressed twice, one the echo of the other, emptiness mirroring emptiness. □

WALL OF SOUND

How a 1987 PERFORMANCE *in Berlin helped unite a country torn apart by* WAR.

› **WORDS** *by* **LUKAS HERMSMEIER**

On June 6, 1987, 70,000 people gathered on the lawn in front of the Reichstag in West Berlin for a three-day concert marking the 750th anniversary of Berlin. They were not very far from the Berlin Wall, which separated the city and ran alongside the Reichstag's eastern wing. It was a symbolic stage for a symbolic artist, and when David Bowie walked out on the evening of the first day—clad head to toe in tomato red—he was ready. On the East German side of the wall, thousands had amassed to hear some rare live Western music. "We knew that people were on the other side. But the wall seemed still unshakable that summer," said Oliver Ohmann, then an 18-year-old high school student watching from the west.

Bowie had visited East Berlin the previous day, prompting an emotional statement in German near the end of the concert: "We send our best wishes to all our friends who are on the other side of the Wall." Bowie was in tears. And so was the audience, who held

sparklers and sang along as he played "'Heroes,'" the Cold War love anthem he'd written in the city a decade earlier.

"Berlin was divided. But the air wasn't," recalls Stephan Krawczyk, a singer and songwriter living in the East banned from publicly performing because of his dissident views. For the East German police, the scene was a provocation. Hundreds of officers tried to clear the streets with water canons and batons while the concertgoers chanted, "Tear down the wall!"

"The sheer force of the police was new to me," Krawczyk says. "I don't want to know how many bones were broken that night." Krawczyk later wrote a song about the riots, including the lines "For some it tasted like popcorn / For others it smelled like rebellion."

In 2002, years after the wall had been torn down and Germany reunified, Bowie gave another concert in Berlin, this time in the East. "So now I was face-to-face with the people I had been singing ["'Heroes'"] to all those years ago," he told an interviewer. "And we were all singing it together. Again, it was powerful. Things like that really give you a sense of what performance can do." □

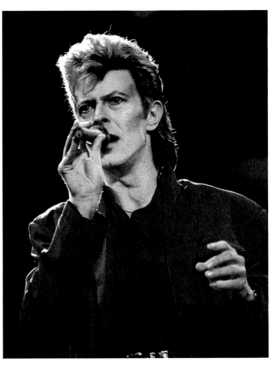

VICTORY IN GERMANY
East Berliners crowd the Reichstag on June 6, 1987; the next night, Bowie played a festival in Nürburg, Germany (right). In a January 11, 2016, tweet, the German Foreign Office thanked the singer "for helping to bring down the wall."

IN THE RED
Aboard the luxury liner
QE2, in Southampton,
U.K., in January 1973.

FASHION

For someone who claimed to hate style but loved to DRESS UP,
Bowie certainly left an incontestable mark on the RUNWAY. *His flair for the
theater of appearance repeatedly* TRANSFORMED *couture and excited
designers with a colorful new* LITANY OF LOOKS.

›PHOTOGRAPH *by* MICK ROCK

ALTERED EGO

In a 2005 interview, an ever-prescient Bowie discusses the EVOLUTION *of his style, the whereabouts of his* FUCK-ME PUMPS, *and the mainstreaming of* ANDROGYNY.

› **WORDS** *by* **DAVE ITZKOFF**
ORIGINALLY PUBLISHED IN *FASHION ROCKS*, FALL 2005
› **PHOTOGRAPH** *by* **HELMUT NEWTON**

Though it's been more than 20 years since he retired his distinctive costumes—the Thin White Duke, Ziggy Stardust, Aladdin Sane—David Bowie is still renowned for his wardrobe choices. In September 2005, he also became a published author with the release of *Moonage Daydream*, which features his commentary on his explosive Ziggy Stardust era, alongside equally provocative photographs by Mick Rock. From his summer home in the Catskills, Bowie spoke about his résumé of stylish alter egos, his sartorial inspirations, and, of course, codpieces.

Can we talk about the intersection of fashion and music in your career?
I'm really not very good at that. Let's talk about new bands!

We'll get to that, I promise you. But I was surprised to see you acknowledge how much Stanley Kubrick's film *A Clockwork Orange* had influenced your Ziggy Stardust look.
Oh yeah. It was impossibly direct. At the time, the film felt like a sledgehammer when it was briefly released in England. It was released for—I believe there were some threats to the Kubrick family, and he pulled the movie very quickly afterward.

Was the controversy of the film what appealed to you?
No, because many controversial films were out at the time. But with that one particularly, it was the aesthetic, the visual aesthetic as much as anything else—the way it looked. The design of the clothes, I thought, was fascinating.

Were you just looking for an excuse to wear a codpiece?
[*Laughs*] Yeah, the codpieces were great. It truly was to bring back a kind of Shakespearean ideal with an exterior item like that. Never to be used again until Cameo's "Word Up." Not the same codpieces, I hope. Also the initial clothes I designed for the Spiders from Mars were very much based on the *Clockwork Orange* jumpsuits. I had them made out of very flowery material, very feminine material, very colorful. I just wanted to—I thought the juxtaposition of the violence inherent in the worker-like clothes with the kind of very soft sensuality of the fabric we chose was an interesting thing to do.

Were there other antecedents to Ziggy that were perhaps less notorious than *A Clockwork Orange*?
There were elements of Kabuki theater thrown in. It was really a hodgepodge; there was no kind of direct through-line with Ziggy at all. It just kind of evolved. I very much had the idea of Japanese culture as the alien culture because I couldn't conceive of a Martian culture.

Is it in any way a negative to acknowledge that a look or a style isn't *sui generis*, that it actually has antecedents?
Oh lord, no. Absolutely not. I've always delved into—I'm terribly analytical about things. I'll always go well into the background of things and find out why they became what they became. That's one of the most interesting things for me about how we live our lives: How did it happen? Not just what it is.

Did you do anything to reacquaint yourself with that era of your life before you began to write the text for *Moonage Daydream*?

TOWERING PRESENCE
Bowie in Monte Carlo, from the November 1983 issue of *Vogue.*

Not really, no. I just kind of used Mick's photographs. There are enough memory clues in them for me personally that I just needed to see a picture of Cyrinda Foxe and I immediately remembered everything about that period. She was fantastic and a huge influence at the time. There was nobody quite like her. And she got me my first fuck-me pumps.

Do you still own those? Are they in a closet somewhere?
I do have them in a box. Actually, a few items were stolen along the way because, I think, they were worth stealing. I don't blame anybody for stealing them at all; I would have. But I've retained a lot of the stuff, and I'm really happy about that.

If it weren't for people stealing things from you, the Sex Pistols would never have had their sound system.
[*Laughs*] You know, [Pistols guitarist] Steve Jones owned up to that. I get on very well with Steve now, but at the time I was extremely angry. Of course, we had no idea who actually stole the stuff.

Now would you think of it more as a borrowing?
An *appropriation*, actually.

How do you know when a look has outlived its usefulness?
For me, it's usually about 10 minutes after I should have gotten rid of it [*laughs*]. I'm always a little late. No, actually, I try to anticipate that it's getting boring, but it's something I don't do so much these days. The outfits I use onstage now are far more functional. It's just to get the show on. I think the major difference, of course, is that I was designing for characters, which I've kind of stopped. I wrapped that up in the early 1980s and didn't do characters after that. Those first years, the Thin White Duke and all those guys, I really was dressing in character. In a way, it was more fun to do, because I find it so boring—ah, I'd much prefer somebody else to just dress me [*laughs*]. Of course, this is not the interview to say that in, is it? But I'm far more interested in the theatrical implications of clothes than I am in everyday fashion.

As you've gotten older, have you found that your sense of style has become more innate?
I'm pleased to say I don't really think about it. I just rely on Hedi Slimane. It's all Dior. I've always been extremely lucky that there's always some designer or other who wants to give me clothes. For the last little while, Hedi Slimane has wardrobed me. I first met him before he became part of Dior, when he sent a bunch of photographs via a friend of mine. The stuff was apparently influenced by the film *The Man Who Fell to Earth*, and it was all that very slim-line black, and it's very much become his key signature look. Now, of course, he's designing for Franz Ferdinand

THE KABUKI INFLUENCE
Bowie incorporated into his stage show elements of traditional Japanese theater, of which this Lincoln Center production of *Summer Festival: A Mirror of Osaka* is one example.

and the Killers. He's doing everybody. He's really changing the look of rock 'n' roll.

Is there a new rock act that, to your mind, carries on the theatrical element that was part of what you did?
Arcade Fire has a very strong theatrical flair, a boisterous, college kind of feel to what they're doing, and also there's a wave of enthusiasm to it. But their show is theatrical nonetheless, because it doesn't alter much from night to night. I've seen them *many* times, and I love them. I think they're exhilarating.

So that was one.
Secret Machines, too, but in a different way. They're almost invisible onstage. The light is behind them, so they're just three dark silhouettes. But the power of their music and of their unseen presence is fantastic. The third one would be TV on the Radio.

How do you keep up with all this new music?
Well, fortunately, I'm not working! [*Laughs*] So I'm resting. I get out a lot. I am a New Yorker, very much, and I get out in New York. It's just a place that I adore. And I love seeing new theater; I love seeing new bands, art shows, everything. I get everywhere—very quietly and never above 14th Street. I'm very downtown.

Of all your collaborators, was there one whose own sense of style intimidated you?
That's an interesting question. The ones I worked with? Nah.

Not even Freddie Mercury?
Oh no. We were worlds apart.

At the end of last year, your music, as sung by a Brazilian musician, played a very significant role in shaping the aesthetic of Wes Anderson's film *The Life Aquatic with Steve Zissou*. Was it at all bittersweet for you that, aside from "Queen Bitch" and "Life on Mars?" it wasn't your voice on the soundtrack?

Oh no! I simply adored that soundtrack album. I thought it was fabulous. I loved that particular take on my work.

How is it that an art like recorded music, which has no visual component, can have such a strong effect on a medium like film, which is all visual?

I don't know! I've got no idea. You answer that. [*Laughs*]

I know you paint as well—has your painting ever influenced your music or vice versa?

They've definitely helped each other. I often find that if I'm hitting some kind of block in my writing, I'll turn to something visual—either go and see other people's work or do some painting of my own. I'll often paint myself into a new perspective on the writing. And often what I'm writing will inspire me to do something visual—it will trigger me to go and paint something.

Do you make it to any of the shows during Fashion Week?

Know something? I've never been to a fashion show in my life.

Really?

No. Iman's world is a complete mystery to me. I've no idea what she was like. I've seen clips of her on the catwalk.

Would it surprise you or disappoint you to know that your song "Fashion" is a staple of these shows?

Well, I know a lot of my music is used. We have to give out licenses for permissions, so it's used all over, frequently in Europe, which I'm very proud of. What am I going to say? [*Laughs*]

This may sound like a very esoteric question, but does the persona of David Jones still exist within you?

Yes. The Bowie character, for me, is strictly to be used for the stage, so I can hide back away again as David Jones. Right now, in the mountains, where I am at the moment, it's David Jones. With my family I'm David Jones, very much.

Is the public ready for androgyny to go mainstream again?

Well, I've noticed there's an element of that in some of the bands, like Franz Ferdinand. You sense that—it's not implicit, but it's sort of hinted at. I'm not sure how important it ever was.

So you're not necessarily the man to carry it forward a second time?

No, no.

If you can ignore the illicit implications, may I ask what you're wearing right now?

Let's see…a white T-shirt and jeans. No shoes, no socks. I'm so David Jones, it's unbelievable.

Have you heard the Futureheads, Bloc Party?

Yeah, and Louis XIV. I tell you, it's just great living in New York, living downtown, going out two or three times a week and catching bands. It's the best thing one can possibly do.

Are you able to get out without drawing attention to yourself?

Well, everybody knows me anyway, and they're very quiet and respectful. New York's New York. Nobody makes a big deal.

Do you still sport the jeans and T-shirt look?

Absolutely. Jeans and a baseball cap. That, frankly, is the way to get around. No stack-heel boots. That would just be asking for trouble. □

COSTUME GALA Performing as Ziggy Stardust, in the "woodland creatures" outfit designed by Kansai Yamamoto, at London's Hammersmith Odeon in 1973.

"IF YOU'RE REALLY GOING TO ENTERTAIN AN AUDIENCE, THEN YOU HAVE TO LOOK THE PART, TOO."

APPROACHING THE BENCH
In Berlin, shortly after starring in the movie *Just a Gigolo* in 1978.

PHOTOGRAPH BY SNOWDON

A SENSE OF STYLE

Bowie's IMPACT *on the world of fashion can never be overstated or undersold. In this portfolio, photographers and designers pay tribute to his uncommon* GENIUS.

———————————

› **WORDS** *by* **RACHEL TASHJIAN**
ORIGINALLY PUBLISHED ON VANITYFAIR.COM, JANUARY 12, 2016

HAIR APPARENT
In the early '70s, rocking the Ziggy Stardust mullet.

David Bowie was less a fashion icon than an embodiment of fashion itself. "Whereas everyone else looked like they were dressing up, Bowie really inhabited those roles," Victoria Broackes, co-curator of "David Bowie is" at London's Victoria and Albert Museum, says. "He really was it." The Kansai Yamamoto space suits of his Ziggy Stardust days presaged the fashion industry's early-'80s obsession with avant-garde Japanese fashion. His dazzling *Aladdin Sane* cover continues in the glittery codes of Olivier Rousteing's Balmain. Gucci's re-imagined dandyism owes a major debt to the *Hunky Dory* years. Hedi Slimane's Saint Laurent rocker waifs are like a drugged-out collage of every '70s Bowie persona. And his Thin White Duke phase flirted with Yves Saint Laurent's dangerously androgynous Le Smoking tuxedo.

While the pop music business historically asks its artists to stick with a formula, Bowie, Broackes argues, "would throw everything up in the air and say, 'Oh no, I'm going to try something else,' and do something different." His perpetual search for difference helped change how we think of celebrity, gender, and even ourselves. "This notion that you have to be only one thing is what he really challenges," Broackes says. "He showed us that we could be many things, sometimes all at the same time."

PHOTOGRAPH BY
CRAIG McDEAN
SASKIA DE BRAUW
W MAGAZINE, 2012

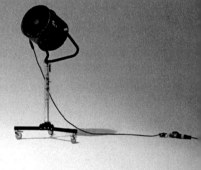

PHOTOGRAPH BY
NICK KNIGHT
KATE MOSS
VOGUE UK, 2003
(Moss is wearing the original
three-piece suit made by Freddie
Burretti and worn by Bowie
in the "Life on Mars?" video.)

PHOTOGRAPH BY
DAVID SIMS
ISELIN STEIRO
VOGUE PARIS, 2010

ONE

TWO

THREE

FOUR

FIVE

SIX

EIGHT

TEN

NINE

ELEVEN

SEVEN

TWELVE

CATWALK PEOPLE

1. Maison Margiela, spring 2016
2. Christian Dior Haute Couture, spring 2015
3. Jean Paul Gaultier, spring 2011
4. Lanvin, fall 2011
5. Givenchy, spring 2010
6. Jean Paul Gaultier, spring 2013
7. Saint Laurent, spring 2014
8. Dries Van Noten, fall 2011
9. Miu Miu, fall 2012
10. Balmain, fall 2011
11. Pam Hogg, fall 2009
12. Walter Van Beirendonck, fall 2013

GOLDEN YEARS

Bowie's life offstage was as much of an ADVENTURE as his life onstage. An autodidact who never stopped searching for NEW EXPERIENCES, he FOUND LOVE after 40 and kept a lifetime of memories hidden in his ever-expanding RECORD COLLECTION.

› **PHOTOGRAPH** *by* **BRIAN ARIS**

Look at the sky, life's begun / Nights are warm and the days are young

DADDY'S HOME
With newborn
daughter Alexandria
Zahra in New York
City, 2000.

In walked luck and you looked in time / Never look back, walk tall, act fine

A PERFECT MATCH

In their own ways, IMAN AND BOWIE *epitomized stardom in the '70s.* TOGETHER *they adjusted to a more* LOW-KEY FAME *in the '90s with a love and marriage that* ENDURED TO THE END.

› **WORDS** *by* **CHARLES GANDEE**
›**PHOTOGRAPH** *by* **IRVING PENN**
ORIGINALLY PUBLISHED IN *VOGUE*, JUNE 1994

The night the model Iman and the pop star David Bowie were introduced by two mutual friends at an Italian restaurant in Los Angeles, their joint fate, they both now confess, was effectively sealed. "David says he was naming the children that night," reports Iman, who is no less direct about her feelings: "I knew immediately that this was my soul mate."

For anyone who remembers the '70s, there is something quite logical about the bond that sprang up so instantly between the legendary model and the legendary pop star, who were married April 24, 1992, in a civil ceremony in Switzerland and then again June 6, 1992, in a church ceremony in Italy. From the moment they strutted onto the world stage—Bowie in 1972, Iman in 1975—their remarkable lives have been remarkably similar.

Throughout the Me Decade and well into the Greed Decade, Iman and Bowie were successfully billed as exotic creatures, verging on the alien. It was as if they were encased in expertly contrived cocoons of mystery, where they breathed some kind of rarefied air that rendered them not simply larger than life, but otherworldly.

Iman has Peter Beard, the photographer who first spotted the then 18-year-old Somalian university student on a Nairobi street in 1975, to thank for the public persona. It was Beard who authored the fable that Iman had been plucked from the jungles of Africa where, depending on the day the story was being told, she was either a shepherdess or a princess. Although not especially original—owing an equal debt to Tarzan, King Kong, and François Truffaut's *The Wild Child*—the story made the desired point. "They thought I didn't speak English," she reports. "I speak five languages." But such niggling details didn't make any difference:

CHEMISTRY SET
"I fell in love with David Jones. I did not fall in love with David Bowie," Iman has said. "Bowie is just a persona. He's a singer, an entertainer."
Bowie and Iman, New York, 1994
© Condé Nast

"David and I aren't really crazy about 'area' rugs."

Bilhuber's mandate, according to his client, was to create a "classic" envelope in which to contain the yin-yang mix of cross-cultural artifacts that Iman and Bowie have collected over the years—including an elaborately painted knee-high wooden phallus that serves as a sword sheath and Japanese wedding chests picked up during the couple's six-week honeymoon in Bali and Kyoto. Bilhuber also supplied the two quicksand-like sofas that are so deep and soft that once you get in it's hard to get out.

"This is the happiest time of my life, because this is the first time that I am happy with my life exactly as it is. Before, I thought, 'Oh, the good old days' or 'Well, I guess the best is yet to come.'"

Although the primary source of Iman's contentment is clearly her marriage, it is telling that when she describes the tie that binds, there is more than a faint echo of the anxiety that inevitably haunts the fantastically famous: "I am totally at ease with him—totally myself. I don't have the feeling that if I reveal something about myself, that something is going to happen to the relationship. I know that whatever he knows of me, he will always be with me."

Things weren't always so enchanted. Certainly they weren't five years ago when, after 14 years in New York, she stopped modeling, ended her four-year relationship with investment banker Will Regan, sold her West Side duplex, and headed to California with Zulekha, her then 10-year-old daughter by former New York Knicks forward Spencer Haywood (whom she married in 1978 and divorced in 1986). "I never looked back," reports Iman, who checked herself and Zulekha into the ever-shabby, ever-chic Chateau Marmont on Sunset Boulevard in Hollywood until she could decide what to do next.

"Before I left Manhattan, I made sure that I could comfortably take care of myself and my child for five years if I didn't work a day," explains Iman, adding, "I was smart; I saved my money, I invested." To what does Iman attribute her financial acumen? "I come from a poor country; I had my family to take care of," she says, noting, with an understandable mixture of pride and relief, that the last of her siblings will graduate from college next year.

The source of Iman's fiscal independence was not only runway and editorial work, but commercial work, including advertising campaigns for, among others, Kenzo, Calvin Klein, and Polished Ambers, a line of cosmetics for black women that Revlon launched in 1975 and discontinued in 1982. She reports that in her best year, financially speaking, she made $2 million. "I could have made much more money," she adds matter-of-factly, "if I weren't black."

If race has been a factor in her professional life, it is not a factor in Iman's personal life. Of her interracial marriage, she says, "I have passed an age, my friend, to be worried about being accepted into 'white' society or 'black' society or any society…. Where do we belong? I think with each other." □

"They just went out and wrote the same sheepherder story." The true story is one that Iman is proud of: "My mother was a nurse, and my father was a teacher. They married very young, and they worked their way up. I would say I was raised middle class, upper middle class." Her father left teaching for diplomacy, ultimately serving as Somalia's ambassador in Saudi Arabia.

Bowie, on the other hand, seems to have masterminded his own fiction. He was the one, you will recall, who sashayed into the spotlight wearing makeup and women's clothes—an eye-catching spectacle that struck a particularly responsive chord in the give-bisexuality-a-chance '70s.

"I didn't marry David Bowie, I married David Jones," explains Iman, who, as you might suspect, is a good judge of the distance between a persona and a person. The David she walked down the aisle with twice is the one who "doesn't read anything past the Renaissance," collects Tintoretto, spends a great deal of time bent over an easel, and leads a quiet life, at least for most of the year, in a "château with a view" in Switzerland, where he reads to her at night.

In the luxe Beverly Hills apartment that represents the first joint domestic venture of her married life (Bowie already owned the château with the view in Switzerland), the second, more-accessible-than-exotic Iman seems right at home. New York decorator Jeffrey Bilhuber has endeavored to age the brand-spanking-new apartment with such instant-patina tricks of the trade as faux-vellum wallpaper and wide-plank ebonized wood floors, which are left bare because, as Iman says,

HEARTS AND MINDS

"He's very English," Iman has said, "in a way that he's a gentleman."

PHOTOGRAPHS BY BRUCE WEBER, FOR *VOGUE*, JUNE 1995

FROM SPACE ODDITY TO RESIDENT ALIEN

In a CANDID *1983 interview with* Mademoiselle, *Bowie talked about what it was like to* COME DOWN TO EARTH *and make* Let's Dance

› **WORDS** *by* **FRANK ROSE**
› **PHOTOGRAPH** *by* **GREG GORMAN**
ORIGINALLY PUBLISHED IN *MADEMOISELLE*, OCTOBER **1983**

Crystalline feaures, hair that varies from blond to orange: There's always been something otherworldly about David Bowie. That's what made him so tantalizing when he burst upon the scene as Ziggy Stardust, exploding every notion of what a rock star was supposed to be. Here was a person who was fragile, fey, and avowedly bisexual, yet he had such a charged presence that those things became suddenly fashionable.

"That does seem to be the end result of a lot of the stuff I did," Bowie admitted in a conversation over lunch in a honky-tonk Manhattan diner. "I did insist on creating an alternative atmosphere in my work. I mean, the majority of the albums that I made were really my trying to present an interesting new landscape. It wasn't an objective vision of this planet or this life at all. I would take great chunks of stuff from this planet and juxtapose that with something chillingly barren and put life against the barrenness and so it produced this third world. But I don't think I was ever really the icy, objective viewer watching in a cold, detached manner. I just felt very much at home in the atmosphere I had created."

Bowie today is a man who's gone through so many identities—glitter god, soul man, space oddity, avant-garde composer—that nobody can quite keep up with him. This David Bowie actually claims to be normal. No more poses, no more disguises, just an all-around entertainer reaching out to people with his art. On the album *Let's Dance*, he dumps the synthesizers for horns and blues guitar and sings songs with titles like "Without You." This from the same star who once presented visions of apocalypse that seemed designed to make William S. Burroughs read like Sunday-school material.

True, he was wearing a polka-dot tie with a green checked shirt and a gray tweed jacket, and his hair, blond this time, had somehow been trained to swoop recklessly across his forehead, but he had an engaging smile and a pleasantly earnest manner. He projected both intelligence and a very definite masculinity; gone was the androgyny of his earlier years.

The joint we met in was an extravaganza of Naugahyde and Formica in the no-man's-land between Times Square and the Hudson River docks—a nitty-gritty sort of place with a mixed clientele of off-duty cabbies and swarthy men in black sunglasses who arrive in limos with New Jersey plates. Bowie comes for the ambience and the anonymity. He also likes the chicken pot pie.

"I never showed my emotions at all when I was a child," he continued. "I closed off tremendously. Yes, I was vulnerable, and a lot of things affected me, but I wouldn't let them show. I was quite cold as a child. But I always had an overriding feeling that I was going to do something worthwhile, although I didn't fully understand what it would be. It was as though I were equipping myself to become a painter or a writer or something without really knowing about it. But I knew I was training for something."

He was a puny youth, ill-suited for the roughness of his surroundings, and he decided early on that he would have to compensate by becoming a superman in a world of his own devising.

"I wanted to present something that fought against the denim feel of the time," he explained between bites of chicken pot pie. "I wanted to worry people—you know, the angry young artist. I was definitely angry at the time—angry because I wasn't recognized as an artist, angry because music sounded so placid and boring and conservative. Nobody was singing my songs and I was really very nervous about going onstage and doing them myself, so the idea of devising a character to sing the songs and then the character

TIE'S THE LIMIT
In 1983, the year he appeared in the movies *Yellowbeard*, *The Hunger*, and *Merry Christmas, Mr. Lawrence*.

"IF YOU WANT TO BE NOTICED, YOU CAN BE, AND IF YOU DON'T WANT TO BE NOTICED, YOU DON'T HAVE TO BE."

becoming part of the album, the whole thing had a logic behind it. That's really when the Ziggy Stardust thing happened."

Bowie ended up becoming the character he'd created—a suicidal pop messiah.

"I partied longer than anybody else, and I did more drugs than anybody else. But you get fed up with waking up at four in the morning, crawling down some street and wondering where the hell you are. Enough years of that and you either go with it to death, or you change."

As an antidote to Los Angeles, where he owned a mansion, Bowie chose Berlin, a city where the poisonous cocoon of superstar existence was not an option. "It was either that or go into a hospital," he said, "and I was intimidated by the stigma of going to a hospital."

Bowie had long felt drawn to Berlin, mainly, he insists, by its heritage as a center of such 20th-century art movements as Expressionism and the Bauhaus. He went with a single friend—Iggy Pop, the punk-rock prototype, who had been trying to kick a drug habit. They rented nearby apartments in the Turkish ghetto and tried to put themselves together again.

"For the first six or seven months, I think I was just adjusting to daily life," Bowie recalled. "You know, small stuff like going out shopping and how to plan a week's worth of groceries, responsibilities which I had given away because one does that in the youthful enthusiasm of being a rock 'n' roll hero. And it was great not having hundreds of people I didn't know in the house all the time, you know. Then, by the end of three years I realized that I had slowly come out of the shell that I had gotten myself in, and I was able to face things in a sane fashion and not worry about pumping myself up with stimulants or whatever to coast through everything."

Bowie reemerged in 1980, cured of any desire to flaunt his stardom or flirt with the edge; from now on, he would play life differently.

"Every few years, I have to redefine what I'm writing," he explained. "I had to do it when I moved to Berlin, and I had to do it again just recently. I had to think, if indeed I want to make another album, do I just want to make another cold album? Is there not another way you can go? So I guess—well, it's a relatively warm album. I mean, for me it's warm." He ducked his head and looked up with a nervous grin, as if expecting flak.

In fact, the Bowie that emerges on *Let's Dance* is playful, suggestive, and, if not exactly warm, at least mindful of the need for human connection.

"The pessimistic message seems so easy to sell these days that I thought it would be heartening to try to respond to that in a positive fashion. So the first thing I did was to take off all the synthesizers, because for me that represents the spearhead of that whole movement.

"Then I thought, what gave me happy feelings? Well, one thing was doing horn arrangements, so I went back to listening to old rhythm-and-blues records—just the innate, enthusiastic quality on them and the wanting to live, and wanting to live in a positive fashion. Why doesn't music sound like that anymore?"

Maybe too many people had been listening to albums like *Ziggy Stardust* and *Scary Monsters*, I suggested. After all, Bowie is hardly in a position to complain about rock nihilism.

"Blame it on Iggy," he said, his face a sudden mask of innocence. "Always blame it on Iggy. Me, nihilistic? Nooo... I was always just a quiet Dadaist."

He broke into a sly grin, then continued in a more serious vein. "I still have to shake that off occasionally, you know—the feeling that nothing matters. You look around you, you see the pointless deaths and greediness and you think, what a hell of a business I'm in, it's really the peak of all greediness and self-centeredness. Why am I doing it? Do I really believe in it? And then I think back to the songs that influenced me and actually meant something to my life and I go, yeah, whatever reasons there were for making those songs, the songs themselves were really important to me."

It was hardly what I'd been expecting to hear—David Bowie talking about music as the beacon of hope. But a few minutes later, a young man came up to our booth. No one else had noticed us, and the man approached us hesitantly. "Excuse me," he said, "but you look so much like David Bowie that—are you David Bowie?"

Bowie sat back and grinned like a cat who'd been caught in the garbage. "A bit. Yeah."

"I don't believe it! Ziggy Stardust!"

Bowie graciously signed an autograph and shook hands—the alien, unreachable star touched briefly. After the fan had left, I asked if strangers approach him often. "No," Bowie said, with an elusive smile. "If you want to be noticed, you can be and if you don't want to be noticed, you don't have to be. Usually, people just think I'm a Bowie clone. And I say, 'What, me? I look nothing like him.'" □

WITH TEETH
Bowie in 1995, the year he released *Outside*.

INFREQUENTLY ASKED QUESTIONS

At 51, rock's CHAMELEON *demonstrated that his* PLAYFULNESS *and taste for* ODDITIES *remained a constant in his life.*

ORIGINALLY PUBLISHED IN *VANITY FAIR*, AUGUST 1998
› **PHOTOGRAPH** *by* **RANKIN**

What is your idea of perfect happiness?
Reading.

What is your most marked characteristic?
Getting a word in edgewise.

What do you consider your greatest achievement?
Discovering morning.

What is your greatest fear?
Converting kilometers to miles.

Which historical figure do you most identify with?
Santa Claus.

Which living person do you most admire?
Elvis.

Who are your heroes in real life?
The consumer.

What is the trait you most deplore in yourself?
While in New York, tolerance. Outside of New York, intolerance.

What is the trait you most deplore in others?
Talent.

What is your favorite journey?
The road of artistic excess.

What do you consider the most overrated virtue?
Sympathy and originality.

Which words or phrases do you most overuse?
"Chthonic," "miasma."

What is your greatest regret?
That I never wore bell-bottoms.

What is your current state of mind?
Pregnant.

If you could change one thing about your family, what would it be?
My fear of them (wife and son excluded).

What is your most treasured possession?
A photograph held together by cellophane tape of Little Richard that I bought in 1958, and a pressed and dried chrysanthemum picked on my honeymoon in Kyoto.

What do you regard as the lowest depth of misery?
Living in fear.

Where would you like to live?
Northeast Bali or south Java.

What is your favorite occupation?
Squishing paint about a senseless canvas.

What is the quality you most like in a man?
The ability to return books.

What is the quality you most like in a woman?
The ability to burp on command.

What are your favorite names?
Sears & Roebuck.

What is your motto?
"What" *is* my motto. □

HIS BARK AND HIS BITE

Upon being named one of British GQ's Men of the Year in 2002, Bowie sounded off on GOD, AMBITION, *family, and 9/11, possibly telling tall tales about* MONKEYS AND JOHN LENNON.

›**WORDS** *by* **DYLAN JONES**
›**PHOTOGRAPHS** *by* **MARKUS KLINKO AND INDRANI**
ORIGINALLY PUBLISHED IN BRITISH *GQ*, OCTOBER 2002

David Bowie is fed up with critics saying he's just produced his best record in ages. It's been happening for years—for so long, in fact, that he treats it as a matter of course. They said it about *Outside*, about *Earthling*, about *'hours…'* and, predictably, they're saying it about *Heathen*. This time, however, Bowie believes them.

"I'm aware it's good work," he says, staring out at Lake Geneva from Le Montreux Palace hotel in Switzerland. "I felt it was a success from the mixing stage. This is a really good album."

Dressed from head to toe in Ralph Lauren ("Everything bar the socks," smiles Bowie), everyone's favorite space bloke is lounging around this particularly rococo hotel having just completed a short European tour that began with his extraordinary concert in London, part of the Meltdown festival he curated at the Southbank Centre in June. As befits a man who is happily married to one of the most beautiful women in the world—Iman, for those of you who tend to spend your lives on Mars—and who has a bouncing 14-month-old daughter, Lexi ("Her first word was 'shoes'!"), David Bowie is demonstrably happy.

And not only has he stopped smoking, it doesn't hurt that he really *has* made his best record in years.

"I would definitely put it up there with some of the better work that I have done, for sure. Although I think it would be easier to say that if the albums were consistently one style. It's the best album at doing what? It's not *Low*. So does that mean that *Low* is my best-ever album? It's not like *Heathen*. *Heathen* is much more a collection of songs, you know? It's more straightforward. So would you compare it to the *Hunky Dory* album? I don't actually think you could. I think they're chalk and cheese.

"I've made over 25 studio albums, and I think probably I've made two real stinkers in my time, and some not-bad albums, and some really good albums. I'm proud of what I've done. In fact it's been a good ride."

In the 30-odd years that Bowie has been a star, he has recorded some of the most important music of the post-Beatles era, and although he is still largely known for the raft of ground-breaking albums he released in the '70s, his work since then has been equally fascinating, and almost as prescient. If you were to compile Bowie's alternative greatest hits, and limited your selection to songs recorded in the last 15 or so years, you'd have a collection of some of his finest work. He is a lifetime away from the androgynous android of the '70s. This was when his ambition and ego were most blind. "I get so much fan mail it has to be handled by a computer," he said in 1976. Computers? What were they? "I'm an instant star. Just add water and stir."

What do you think people most misunderstand about you?

What's to misunderstand? I mean, honestly, I'm just a

MANIPULATOR
These pictures were created using intricate digital montage, merging head shots of Bowie with photos of a model dressed by the singer's regular stylist.

bloke doing his job, and it's not terribly complicated. What I do is I write mainly about very personal and rather lonely feelings, and I explore them in a different way each time. You know, what I do is not terribly intellectual. I'm a pop singer for Christ's sake. As a person, I'm fairly uncomplicated. I don't need very much—I'm not needy in that way. I'm not as driven as I once was.

If you don't have the drive, has having a family curtailed your thirst for culture?
No. There's more of a joy in the way that I explore day-to-day existence than there was before. I mean, it was changing for me personally even before Iman came along; it's not like it's sort of all come together just because of the family. The family has come together because of what's been happening to me.

I'll tell you what a lot of it is: It's moving from a life of action to one a little more of contemplation. Initially every minute of your life has to count, and you have to be doing something. I think that I'm not quite like that anymore. Possibly because both my parents had the same work-ethic thing—you know, work as salvation. The humanists' replacement for religion: work really hard and somehow you'll either save yourself or you'll be immortal. Of course, that's a total joke, and our progress is nothing. There may be progress in technology, but there's no ethical progress whatsoever; we're still exactly the same immoral bastards that we were 20,000 years ago. You start to feel that maybe ▶ *continued on page 106*

"THE ONLY WAY TO BREAK NEW GROUND IS TO BE PREPARED TO PUT AN AWFUL LOT AT RISK."

SMOKE SIGNAL
In 1974, at a TV studio in Holland, where he played "Rebel, Rebel."

PHOTOGRAPH BY BARRY SCHULTZ

"I AM A D.J., I AM WHAT I PLAY"

In 2003, Bowie told Vanity Fair *the* STORIES *behind 25 of his greatest* DISCOVERIES, *from his collection of 2,500* VINYL *albums.*

› **WORDS** *by* **DAVID BOWIE**
ORIGINALLY PUBLISHED IN *VANITY FAIR*, NOVEMBER **2003**

ORANGE CRUSH
Bowie in 1976.

There is really no way to do a list of my favorite albums with any rationality. I do only have about 2,500 vinyls. There is a possibility there. I'll look through the albums and pull together a list of those I have rebought or am in the process of re-buying on CD. I have little time, and there are just too many to sort through. So, I'll keep pulling stuff out blindly, and if it's too obvious (*Sgt. Pepper*, Nirvana) I'll put it back again till I find something more interesting. A lot of the rock stuff I have is the same as everyone else's, and I have so many blues and R&B albums that it would topple over into trainspotter world if I went that route.

O.K., no rules then. I'll just make 'em up as I go along. I'd say half of this list is now on my CD racks, but many are finding impossible to trace. The John Lee Hooker album, for instance, or *The Red Flower of Tachai Blossoms Everywhere*. I have done the only thing possible and burned them to CD myself, reduced the cover art down to size, and made reasonable simulacrums of the originals.

If you can possibly get your hands on any of these, I guarantee you evenings of listening pleasure, and you will encourage a new high-minded circle of friends, although one or two choices will lead some of your old pals to think you completely barmy. So, without chronology, genre, or reason, herewith, in no particular order, 25 albums that could change your reputation.

THE LAST POETS
THE LAST POETS
(1970, Douglas)
One of the fundamental building blocks of rap. All the essential "griot" narrative skills, splintered with anger here, produce one of the most political vinyls to ever crack the Billboard chart. While talking rap (what?), I can piggyback this great treat with the 1974 compilation *The Revolution Will Not Be Televised* (Flying Dutchman), which pulls together the best of the formidable Gil Scott-Heron works.

"SHIPBUILDING"
ROBERT WYATT
(1982, Rough Trade)
Not an album, a 12-inch single. A vinyl nonetheless. A well-thought-through and relentlessly affecting song co-written by Elvis Costello, and Wyatt's interpretation is the definitive. Heartbreaking—reduces strong men to blubbering girlies.

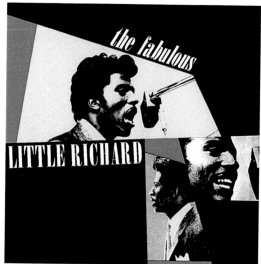

THE FABULOUS LITTLE RICHARD
LITTLE RICHARD
(1959, Specialty)
Unusually subdued, these performances were recorded by Richard at his first Specialty sessions, mostly in 1955. It was sold to me discount by Jane Greene. More of her later.

MUSIC FOR 18 MUSICIANS
STEVE REICH
(1978, ECM)
Bought in New York. Balinese gamelan music cross-dressing as Minimalism. Saw this performed live in downtown New York in the late '70s. All white shirts and black trousers. Having just finished a tour in white shirt and black trousers, I immediately recognized Reich's huge talent and great taste. The music (and the gymnastics involved in executing Reich's tag-team approach to shift work) floored me. Astonishing.

THE VELVET UNDERGROUND & NICO
THE VELVET UNDERGROUND
(1967, Verve)
Brought back from New York by a former manager of mine, Ken Pitt. Pitt had done some kind of work as a P.R. man that had brought him into contact with the Factory. Warhol had given him this coverless test pressing (I still have it, no label, just a

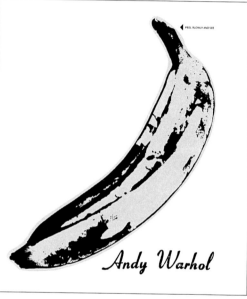

small sticker with Warhol's name on it) and said, "You like weird stuff—see what you think of this." What I "thought of this" was that here was the best band in the world. In December of 1966, my band Buzz broke up, but not without my demanding we play "I'm Waiting for the Man" as one of the encore songs at our last gig. Amusingly, not only was I to cover Velvet's song before anyone else in the world, I actually did it before the album came out. Now that's the essence of mod.

THE FOLK LORE OF JOHN LEE HOOKER
JOHN LEE HOOKER
(1961, Vee Jay)
By 1963, I was working as a junior commercial artist at an advertising agency in London. My immediate boss, Ian, a groovy modernist with Gerry Mulligan-style short crop haircut and Chelsea boots, was very encouraging about my passion for music, something he and I both shared, and used to send me on errands to Dobell's Jazz record shop on Charing Cross Road knowing I'd be there for most of the morning till well after lunch break. It was there, in the "bins," that I found Bob Dylan's first album. Ian had sent me there to get him a John Lee Hooker release and advised me to pick up a copy for myself, as it was so wonderful. Within weeks my pal George Underwood and I had changed the name of our little R&B outfit to the Hooker Brothers and had included both Hooker's "Tupelo" and Dylan's version of "House of the Rising Sun" in our set. We added drums to "House," thinking we'd made some kind of musical breakthrough, and were understandably gutted when the Animals released the song to stupendous reaction. Mind you, we had played our version live only twice, in tiny clubs south of the river Thames, in front of 40 or so people, not one of whom was an Animal. No nicking, then!

BLUES, RAGS AND HOLLERS
KOERNER, RAY AND GLOVER
(1963, Elektra)
Bought at Dobell's. In his own way, "Spider" John Koerner was an influence on Bob Dylan, with whom he used to play in the coffee bars of Dinkytown, the arty section around the University of Minnesota. Demolishing the puny vocalizations of "folk" trios like the Kingston Trio and Peter, Paul and Whatsit, Koerner and company showed how it should be done. First time I had heard a 12-string guitar.

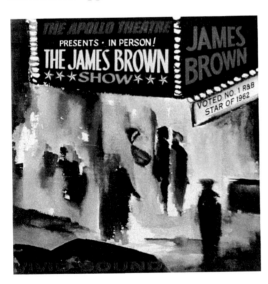

THE APOLLO THEATRE PRESENTS: IN PERSON! THE JAMES BROWN SHOW
JAMES BROWN
(1963, King)
My old schoolmate Geoff MacCormack brought this around to my house one afternoon, breath-

less and overexcited. "You have never, in your life, heard anything like this," he said. I made a trip to see Jane Greene that very afternoon. Two of the songs on this album, "Try Me" and "Lost Someone," became loose inspirations for Ziggy's "Rock & Roll Suicide." Brown's Apollo performance still stands for me as one of the most exciting live albums ever. Soul music now had an undisputed king.

FORCES OF VICTORY
LINTON KWESI JOHNSON
(1979, Mango)
A Carib-Brit contribution to the history of rap. This man writes some of the most moving poetry to be found in popular music. The quite achingly sad "Sonny's Lettah (Anti-Sus Poem)" is alone worth the price of admission. Although not sung but spoken word set against a superb band, this must be one of the most important reggae records of all time. I gave my original copy just recently to Mos Def, in whom I see connections to Johnson, thinking I had already got it on CD. Dammit, I haven't. So now I'm searching high and low for a copy.

THE RED FLOWER OF TACHAI BLOSSOMS EVERYWHERE: MUSIC PLAYED ON NATIONAL INSTRUMENTS
VARIOUS ARTISTS
(1972, China Record Company)
How can you not love music with selections titled "Delivering Public-Grain to the State" or "Galloping Across the Vast Grasslands" (a real foot tapper, that one). Apart from reading like outtakes from a Brian Eno album, these tracks are actually rather lovely examples of folkish music played on traditional instruments. I bought about 20 different 10-inchers of this genre at ridiculously low prices at a Chinese woodblock print fair in Berlin in the late '70s. The cover art proudly

displays a smart and highly functional–looking hydroelectric dam, similar to but presumably smaller than the one which is now flooding hundreds of villages on either side of the glorious Yangtze River. Nice pastel colors, though, and classy white-gold print.

BANANA MOON
DAEVID ALLEN
(1971, BYG Actuel)
It's possible, just possibly maybe, that strands of the embryonic glam style started here. I replayed it just this morn-

ing and was flabbergasted to hear something that sounds like Bryan Ferry and the Spiders from Mars (together, at last!!) on Track 1, recorded a full year before the "official" glam releases from either of the two above-mentioned protagonists. There are, however, no doubts about Allen and fellow band member Robert Wyatt's huge influence on the more "high-minded" layers of pop with their protean unit, the Soft Machine. Allen had, a few years earlier, formed the loony Gong. Wyatt went on to a long and respected solo career, intermittently working with ex-Roxyite Brian Eno.

JACQUES BREL IS ALIVE AND WELL AND LIVING IN PARIS
CAST ALBUM
(1968, CBS)
In the mid-'60s, I was having an on-again, off-again thing with a wonderful singer-songwriter who had previously been the girlfriend of Scott Walker. Much to my chagrin, Walker's music played in her apartment night and day. I sadly lost contact with her, but unexpectedly kept a fond and hugely admiring love for Walker's work. One of the writers he covered on an early album was Jacques Brel. That was enough to take me to the theater to catch the above-named production

when it came to London in 1968. By the time the cast, led by the earthy translator and Brooklynite Mort Shuman, had gotten to the song that dealt with guys lining up for their syphilis shots ("Next"), I was completely won over. By way of Brel, I discovered French chanson a revelation. Here was a popular song form wherein poems by the likes of Sartre, Cocteau, Verlaine, and Baudelaire were known and embraced by the general populace. No flinching, please.

ELECTRONIC MUSIC
THE ELECTROSONIKS
(1962, Vendor Philips)
This was one of those strange albums put out by the record companies to show off that newfangled stereo. Only, here Philips opted for a truly pioneering couple of Dutch bods, Tom Dissevelt and Kid Baltan. As sonic explorers, these two rate along with Ennio Morricone, but far loopier. I'd adore a 5.1 mix of these absurdities. The sleeve notes inform us that "chimpanzees are painting, gorillas are writing." Way to go.

THE 5000 SPIRITS OR THE LAYERS OF THE ONION
THE INCREDIBLE STRING BAND
(1967, Elektra)
O.K., here's the album with the trippiest cover. Color's all over the place on this one, a real eye dazzler. Probably executed by the art group known as "the Fool." Pretty much locked into a time capsule for many years—it's uplifting to find that this strange assortment of Middle Eastern and Celtic folk-mystic stuff stands up remarkably well now. A summer-festival "must" in the '60s, myself and T. Rexer Marc Bolan both being huge fans.

TEN SONGS BY TUCKER ZIMMERMAN
TUCKER ZIMMERMAN
(1969, Regal Zonophone/ EMI)
Now there's a title with

cool clarity. The guy's way too qualified for folk, in my opinion. Degrees in theory and composition, studying under composer Henry Onderdonk, Fulbright scholarship, and he wants to be Dylan. A waste of an incendiary talent? Not in my opinion. I always found this album of stern, angry compositions enthralling, and often wondered what ever happened to him. Tucker, an American, was one of the first artists to be produced by my friend and co-producer Tony Visconti, also an American, after they found each other in London. I wonder? Ah, yup, he's got a website. Lives in Belgium. Look him up.

RICHARD STRAUSS: FOUR LAST SONGS
GUNDULA JANOWITZ
(1974, Deutsche Grammophon)
Like that certain book, this is one album that I give to friends and acquaintances continually. Although Eleanor Steber and Lisa Della Casa do fine interpretations of this monumental work, Janowitz's performance of Strauss's *Four Last Songs* has been described,

rightly, as transcendental. It aches with love for a life that is quietly fading. I know of no other piece of music, nor any performance, which moves me quite like this.

THE ASCENSION
GLENN BRANCA
(1981, 99 Records)
Bought in Zurich, Switzerland. This was an impulse buy. The cover got me. Robert Longo produced what is essentially the best cover art of the '80s (and

beyond, some would say). Mysterious in the religious sense, Renaissance angst dressed in Mugler. And on the inside... Well, what at first sounds like dissonance is soon assimilated as a play on the possibilities of overtones from massed guitars. Not Minimalism, exactly—unlike La Monte Young and his work within the harmonic system, Branca uses the overtones produced by the vibration of a guitar string. Amplified and reproduced by many guitars simultaneously, you have an effect akin to the drone of Tibetan Buddhist monks but much, much, much louder. Two key players in Branca's band were future composer David Rosenbloom (the terrific *Souls of Chaos*, 1983) and Lee Ranaldo, founding figure with Thurston Moore of the great Sonic Youth. Over the years, Branca got even louder and more complex than this, but here on the title track his manifesto is already complete.

THE MADCAP LAUGHS
SYD BARRETT
(1970, Harvest/EMI)
Syd will always be the Pink Floyd for some of us older fans. He made this album, according to legend, while fragile and precariously out of control. Malcolm Jones, one of his producers at the time, denies this vehemently. I will go with Jones, as he was there. Highlight track for me is "Dark Globe," gloriously disturbing and poignant all at once.

BLACK ANGELS
GEORGE CRUMB
(1972, CRI)
Bought in New York, mid-'70s. Probably one of the only concert pieces inspired by the Vietnam War. But it is also a study in spiritual annihilation. I heard this piece for the first time in the darkest time of my own '70s, and it scared the bejabbers out

of me. At the time, Crumb was one of the new voices in composition and Black Angels one of his most chaotic works. It's still hard for me to hear this piece without a sense of foreboding. Truly, at times, it sounds like the devil's own work.

FUNKY KINGSTON
TOOTS & THE MAYTALS
(1973, Dragon)
If you fancy yourself as a bit of a reggae nut, you will have this, of course. Toots Hibbert claimed me with his powerful "Pressure Drop" contribution to the *Harder They Come* soundtrack in the early '70s. Then followed this fantastic and truly funky album in 1973. I was living on a street off the quite gentrified Cheyne Walk in London, and for the first time I started getting complaints from neighbors about the volume I played my records at, this

beauty being the main culprit. Hibbert, by the way, claims to be "the Inventor of Reggae." Nice one, Toots.

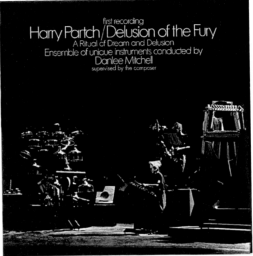

DELUSION OF THE FURY
HARRY PARTCH
(1971, Columbia)
Bought in London at HMV, Oxford Street. I have only the haziest memory of when I first heard of this guy. I believe that it was Tony Visconti, my oft-times producer, who clued me in. A madman of sorts and certainly a onetime hobo, Partch set about inventing and making dozens of the most extraordinary instruments. (When was the last time you saw someone playing the Bloboy, the Eucal Blossom, or the Spoils of War? How do you tune a Spoils of War?, I wonder.) Then, between the 1930s and the 1970s, he wrote wondrous and evocative compositions for them, his subjects ranging from mythology to days riding the trains during the Depression. Delusion represents the best overview of what Partch got up to. By turns creepy as hell and positively rocking. Hav-

ing chosen a musical path that departed from the mainstream composers, he laid the ground for people like Terry Riley and La Monte Young.

OH YEAH
CHARLES MINGUS
(1962, Atlantic)
In the early '60s, Medhurst's was the biggest department store in Bromley, my British hometown. In terms of style, they were to be pulverized by their competitors down the road, who stocked up early on the new, G Plan, Scandinavian-style furniture. But Medhurst's did have, unaccountably, a fantastic record department, run by a wonderful "married" couple, Jimmy and Charles. There wasn't an American release they didn't have or couldn't get. Quite as hip as any London supplier. I would have had a very dry musical run were it not for this place. Jane Greene, their counter assistant, took a liking to me, and whenever I would pop in, which was most afternoons after school, she would let me play records in the "sound

booth" to my heart's content till the store closed at 5:30 P.M. Jane would often join me, and we would smooch big-time to the sounds of Ray Charles or Eddie Cochran. This was very exciting, as I was around 13 or 14 and she would be a womanly 17 at

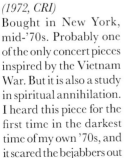

that time. My first older woman. Charles let me buy at a huge discount, enabling me to build up a fab collection over the two or three years that I frequented this store. Happy days. Jimmy, the younger partner, recommended this Mingus album one day around 1962. I lost my original Medhurst copy, but have continued to re-buy the print through the years, as it was re-released time and time again. It has on it the rather give-away track "Wham Bam Thank You Ma'am." It was also my introduction to Roland Kirk.

LE SACRE DU PRINTEMPS
IGOR STRAVINSKY
(1960, MFP/EMI)

For me, a classic example of the eye doing the buying. Excuse the pun. In the late '50s, Woolworth's sold a cheap series of classical albums on the Music for Pleasure label. I spotted this one in the racks and was so taken with the photo of the mountain (Ayers Rock in Australia, as it turned out) that resistance was impossible. With help from the liner notes, which I found incredibly illuminating, I could almost construct my own imagined dance to this fantastic piece of music. The ostinato theme for the tuba is as powerful a riff as any found in rock. Earlier in my then short life I had bought Gustav Holst's *The Planets* suite, motivated by watching a tremendous sci-fi series on BBC television called *The Quatermass Experiment* from behind the sofa when my parents thought I had gone to bed. After each episode

I would tiptoe back to my bedroom rigid with fear, so powerful did the action seem to me. The title music was "Mars, the Bringer of War," so I already knew that classical music wasn't boring.

THE FUGS
THE FUGS
(1966, ESP)

The sleeve notes were written by Allen Ginsberg and contain these perennial yet prescient lines:

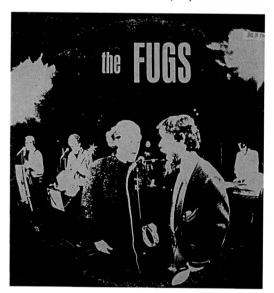

"Who's on the other side? People who think we are bad. Other side? No, let's not make it a war, we'll all be destroyed, we'll go on suffering till we die if we take the War Door." I found on the Internet the text for a newsprint ad for the Fugs, who, coupled with the Velvet Underground, played the April Fools Dance and Models

Ball at the Village Gate in 1966. The FBI had them on their books as "the Fags." This was surely one of the most lyrically explosive underground bands ever. Not the greatest musicians in the world, but how "punk" was all that? Tuli Kupferberg, Fugs co-writer and performer, in collaboration with Ed Sanders, has just finished the new Fugs album as I write. Tuli is 80 years old.

THE GLORY (????) OF
THE HUMAN VOICE
FLORENCE FOSTER JENKINS
(1962, RCA)

In the mid- to late '70s, Norman Fisher, art and people collector, threw the most diverse soirées in the whole of New York. People from every sector of the so and not so avant-garde would flock to his tiny downtown apartment just because Norman was a magnet. Charismatic, huge fun, and brilliant at introducing all the right people to the wrong people. His musical taste was as frothy as he himself. Two of his recommendations have stayed with me over the years. One was *Manhattan Tower*, the first radio mu-

sical by Gordon Jenkins (no relation to Florence), and the other *The Glory (????) of the Human Voice*. Madame Jenkins was rich, social, and devoted to opera. She had, and was blissfully unaware of, the worst set of pipes in the world of music. She would grace the New York set with this monstrous voice once or twice a year with private recitals at the Ritz-Carlton for the lucky few. So popular were these affairs that the tickets were scalped for outrageous prices. To meet the demand, Madame eventually hired Carnegie Hall. This was the hot ticket of that year, 1944. Everyone was there, falling into the aisles in barely suppressed hysterics. During one performance of the song "Clavelitos," Madame, who would change costume at least three times during the course of a recital, became so carried away punctuating the cadences of the song by tossing tiny red flowers from a basket that the basket itself, in her enthusiasm, followed the flowers into the lap of a delighted fan. Be afraid, be very afraid. □

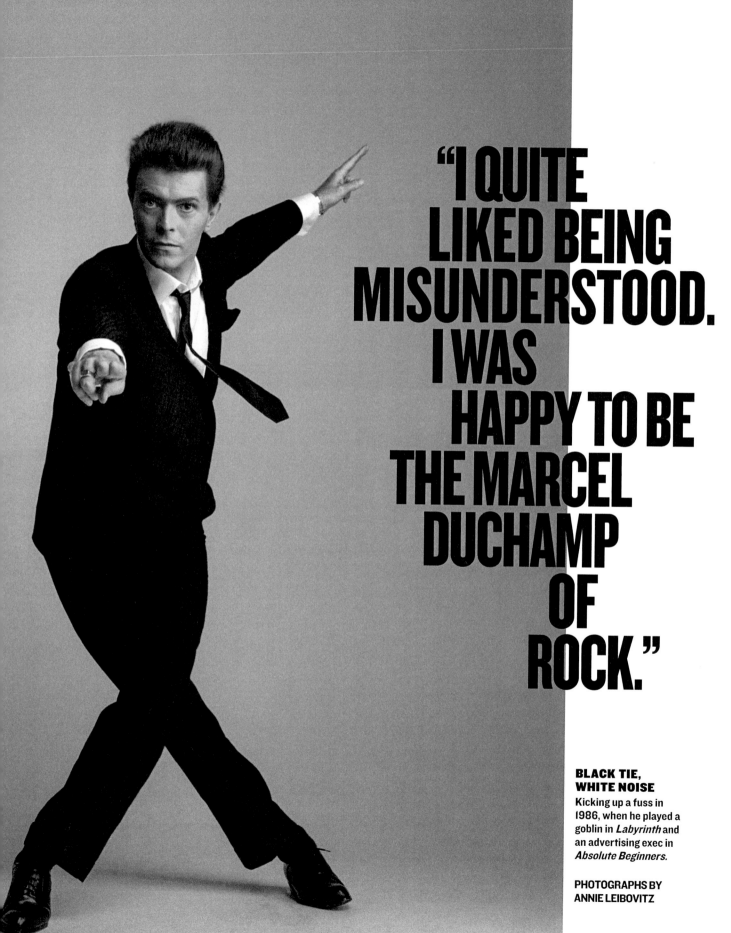

"I QUITE LIKED BEING MISUNDERSTOOD. I WAS HAPPY TO BE THE MARCEL DUCHAMP OF ROCK."

BLACK TIE, WHITE NOISE
Kicking up a fuss in 1986, when he played a goblin in *Labyrinth* and an advertising exec in *Absolute Beginners*.

PHOTOGRAPHS BY ANNIE LEIBOVITZ

SOUND AND VISION

Bowie's ARTISTIC IMPULSES *were too broad and restless for any*
one medium. His SEARCH FOR INSPIRATION *led him to create music that*
STIMULATED *the mind and the body and movies that merged the*
UNREAL *with the* SURREAL—*becoming a* PIONEER *of the modern music video.*

›PHOTOGRAPH *by* MARIO TESTINO

And I will sing, waiting for the gift of sound and vision / Drifting into my solitude, over my head

PIANO MAN
The singer (seen here in 2002) also played the visible keyboard, guitar, drums, and saxophone, among other instruments.

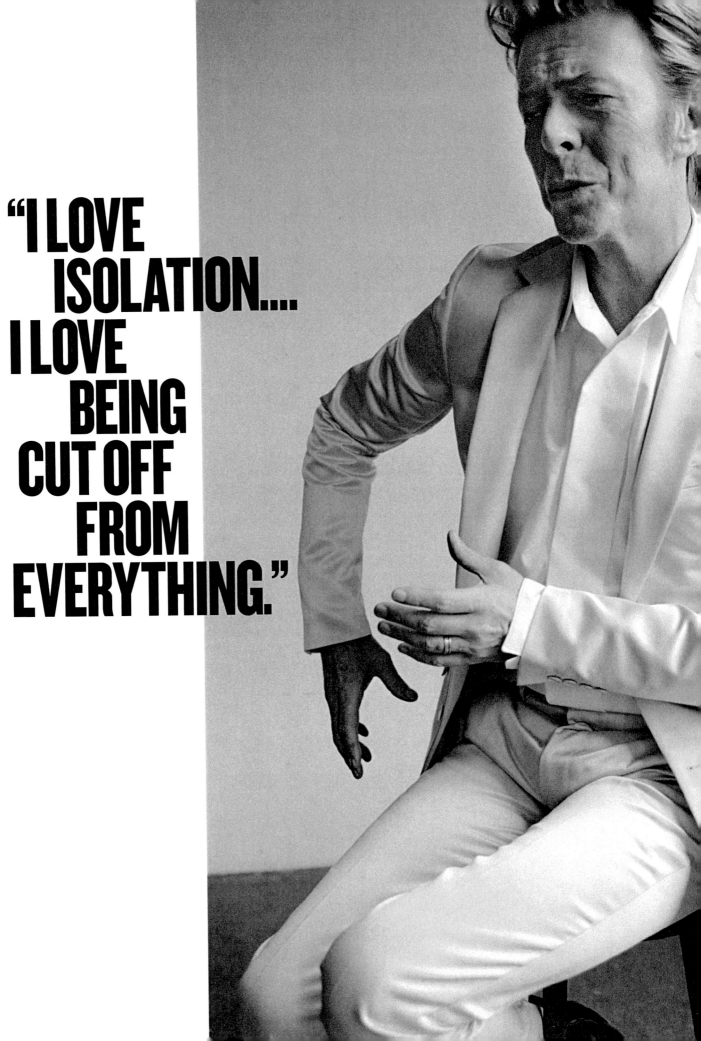

"I LOVE ISOLATION.... I LOVE BEING CUT OFF FROM EVERYTHING."

A MAN OF THE MOVIES

Labyrinth. Just a Gigolo. A Knight's Tale.
Bowie could be an OVERWHELMING PRESENCE *in films—even when he was* NOWHERE *to be found onscreen.*

› **WORDS** *by* **ANTHONY LANE**

ORIGINALLY PUBLISHED ON NEWYORKER.COM, JANUARY 13, 2016

A road at night, unreeling before our eyes. Dashed yellow line down the center, flickering by at unmanageable speed. Yellow lettering to match it, rushing toward us, bearing names that scatter and burst. Blue-gray blur of headlights on the asphalt; we must be in a vehicle, though we see no driver, no wipers, and no steering wheel. And a sound of equal velocity: drums and guitar, then a voice that keens—light and high, ungrand, yet with something urgent to impart: "Funny how secrets travel / I'd start to believe / If I were to bleed /Thin skies / The man chains his hands held high / Cruise me blond / Cruise me babe…" How come we haven't crashed yet? What about those secrets? Is there really a blond? Where are the oncoming cars?

That is the start of David Lynch's *Lost Highway* (1997), one of the most exciting credit sequences that cinema has thrown in our direction; the audience is left shaking before the story has even begun. As for the voice, it belongs to David Bowie. The song is "I'm Deranged," which he wrote, with Brian Eno, for the 1995 album *Outside*. We will hear it again at the end of the movie, by which time Lynch will have made quite sure, as is his custom, that derangement has wafted through the auditorium like a dose of the flu. *Lost Highway* seems to cruise along according to Bowie's instructions, as if determined to prove that the mysteries of which he sang were true. The film veers all over the place, but he shows it the way.

Bowie, who died on January 10, at the age of 69, was a man of the movies. That is not to say that he was a great actor—at least, not on the big screen—nor that

most of the films in which he appeared were anything but minor. But his career, so conscientiously self-wrought, was more akin to that of a movie star than to that of a rocker, and it also suggested that he grasped the force of the moving image, and its fragile half-life, more acutely than many of those who bestride the dramatic profession. "What do you think I'm like?," he asked Dick Cavett, who was interviewing him in 1974. "A working actor," Cavett said. "That's very good," his guest, who had yet to appear in a feature film, replied.

He *had* appeared in *Ziggy Stardust and the Spiders from Mars*, D.A. Pennebaker's documentary (shot the year before), which caught the unpredicted moment, onstage in London, when Bowie announced the death—somewhere between a retirement and a vanishing act—of the Ziggy persona. To listen to some of the tributes paid after Bowie's actual death, you might think that Bowie had spent most of his earthly span in a jumpsuit of many colors, or in other varieties of extraterrestrial garb, whereas the sobering fact is that the Ziggy Stardust tour lasted a mere 17 months. Questioned, early on, about his quicksilver style, Bowie said, "It's like looking at an actor's films, and taking clippings from the films, and saying, 'Here he is.'" Notice the stress on the clip. Well before the advent of the music video (another short form that he mastered), and decades before YouTube, Bowie foresaw that our taste, and our impatient appetites, would beckon us toward the fragmentary. He had the courage of his own brevity, being not just canny enough to leave his fans aching for more but wise enough to know that the incandescent glow of a look is all the more enduring, on the public retina, for being snuffed out. Then he paused, relit himself as something else, and carried on.

That can happen in the movies, too, but seldom is it the prerogative of the star. It was a shock to the

HIS AIM IS TRUE
Playing a brother from another planet, Bowie shoots to thrill in *The Man Who Fell to Earth.*

worshippers of Rita Hayworth when her rolling red tresses were snipped off, for *The Lady from Shanghai* (1947), and replaced by a curt blond crop. But the man who ordered the scissors was the director, Orson Welles, whereas the Bowie who made the same transition, from the gravity-spurning russet quiff of Ziggy to the bright, almost Tintin-like forelock of the "Let's Dance" era, in the 1980s, was directing himself.

How screen performers must crave the command that Bowie asserted over his own transmutations, and envy the fruits that he plucked from new technology. Where a movie star, immured in a blockbuster, might struggle for creative space and fret, with justice, about being overrun by digital tricks, Bowie realized that he could use the Internet to slip in and out of our consciousness, like a guest or an amicable ghost. With films such as *12 Years a Slave*, *The Great Beauty*, and *Blue Is the Warmest Color*, 2013 was not a bad year for the cinema, but none of those movies, I think, had the sudden impact that was made by Bowie's "Where Are We Now?"—the song that fell to earth, unheralded and unhyped, on January 8th. "Just walking the dead," he sang, without fanfare or ado, like a man out walking his dog. Stories were told of grown men switching on their radios, hearing that new cry from a familiar voice, and being stirred to the brink of tears. And all without the slow grind of a marketing campaign; set beside the mercurial business of Bowie, the movie industry appears to be forged from lead.

Hence, perhaps, the tug of dissatisfaction that we feel when surveying the sprawl of his films. I remember being more thrilled by the prospect of Bowie as Pontius Pilate, in Martin Scorsese's *The Last Temptation of Christ* (1988), than I was by the result. As for *Just a Gigolo* (1978), the promise delivered by the poster—Bowie

LEADING MAN
Bowie tangles with his vampire lover, played by Catherine Deneuve, in 1983's *The Hunger* (above), and tangos with Kim Novak in *Just a Gigolo*. Jonathan Rhys Meyers peacocks as a Bowie-like performer in *Velvet Goldmine* (opposite page).

and Marlene Dietrich, together onscreen!—was unfulfilled, not just because the movie was dire but also, it transpired, because they never had been together. Their scenes were shot separately and merged. In our imaginations, though, how tempting the union remains—the native Berliner and the starved-looking Briton who would make his home in that city, and put it to such remarkable purpose, amid the frost of the Cold War. It was Dietrich who, in a nightclub scene from *Morocco* (1930), wore a top hat, white tie, and tails, strolled up to a table, and kissed a woman on the mouth. Tell me Bowie did not learn from that.

There were other calamities, too, from which Bowie, ever the escapologist, managed to flee unscathed, and even with his reputation—or his catalogue of hits—enhanced. Nobody, nowadays, recalls much of *Absolute Beginners* (1986), and rightly so, but the whole enterprise was worth it for the title song that Bowie provided—for the single chord, to be honest, that strikes between the first and second lines of the verse: "I've nothing much to offer / There's nothing much to take." But why are we struck so? What is it in the echo of that strum that refuses to go away? In a word, surprise. Time and again, whether in the symphonic flourishes of his dress-sense or in the choice of one note, Bowie perceived our expectations and swerved aside. He grew weary, it is alleged, of the Serious Moonlight tour, in 1983, and perplexed by the pitch of fame that it brought, but I cannot forget the Shakespearean shock of hearing that adjective for the first time, on "Let's Dance." Moonlight had always been gentle, or flattering, or soft; it was the stuff of sonatas and

serenades. But who knew that it could be serious, like an ailment or an affair of state?

It was on a previous tour, for *Station to Station*, in 1976, that Bowie had screened passages from *Un Chien Andalou* onstage. There could be few better guides to Bowie's instinct; that 1929 movie, directed by Luis Buñuel and Salvador Dalí—despite its running time, barely more than twenty minutes—remains a bible of the unexpected. As for the design of the shows, Bowie confessed to his candid borrowings from German expressionist film, plus "the lighting of, say, Fritz Lang or [G.W.] Pabst." Considering this addiction to chop and change, and to the mustering of sound and vision into a restless collage, it may be inevitable that, when Bowie did assume substantial roles, in other people's films, he seemed less light on his feet. He was required to sustain a character, and to lend it an arc, whereas his natural tendency, given any arc, was to bend it or snap it in two. Movies are the bedmates of poetry, as Bowie knew, and to treat them as a sort of illustrated novel is to load them with a burden they were scarcely designed to bear. Thus, his cameo in *Zoolander*, whipping off his shades and guying his own status as a lionized legend beside the catwalk, is not only more entertaining, but more tightly bound to Bowiehood, than his entire leading role in *Merry Christmas, Mr. Lawrence*. If, back in 1983, you could open a magazine, find the startling image, from that movie, of his fair imprisoned head (he is buried up to his neck, like the heroine of Beckett's *Happy Days*), cut it out and stick it up on your wall, you had what you needed, and no more.

One drawback to Bowie on film, strange to say, was his speaking voice. Deployed to such astonishing effect, be it chatty or percussive, within his songs, ("I know when to go out, / And when to stay in," he reveals, in a low, confiding murmur, at the kickoff of "Modern Love"), it was curiously floated and flattened by motion pictures. That is as evident in his Nikola Tesla, in Christopher Nolan's *The Prestige* (2006), as it was in his Goblin King, in *Labyrinth* (1986), where he boasted a magnificent wig that might have been plugged into one of Tesla's experiments. Jim Henson's film, half-derided at the time, has since acquired a fond following, but it must be admitted that few of Bowie's line readings, for any director, resound with a fraction of the ululating bark with which he powers through the spoken verses of "The Jean Genie." One hesitates to say this of a rock god, but he might have made better films in the silent age.

The exception, needless to say, is *The Man Who Fell to Earth*, Nicolas Roeg's indomitably weird creation of 1976, which ravened up "Space Oddity," "Starman," "Life on Mars?," and every other scrap of Bowie's otherworldliness to conjure its disaffected fable. Bowie plays Thomas Newton, an alien who comes to us not in peace, nor to make war, but in search of water. He stays, invents, discovers alcohol and sex, grows wealthy, gets trapped and preyed upon, and never leaves. The melancholy of that final ▶ **continued on next page**

TEENAGE KICKS

The director of Velvet Goldmine *on the* IMPACT *of Bowie and glam rock.*

› **WORDS** *by* **JOANNA ROBINSON**
ORIGINALLY PUBLISHED ON VANITYFAIR.COM, JANUARY 11, 2016

In 1998 Todd Haynes made *Velvet Goldmine*—a dazzling examination of the emergence of gender-bending glam rock with characters that were clearly based on Iggy Pop (Ewan McGregor) and David Bowie (Jonathan Rhys Meyers). Bowie's influence can be seen throughout Haynes's body of work. The clear through line is the rejection of societal expectations of identity. It's true of the female lovers in *Carol*, it's true of the shape-shifting Bob Dylan in *I'm Not There*, and it's front and center in period pieces like *Mildred Pierce* and *Far from Heaven*.

In a conversation with Marc Maron that aired three days before the singer's death, Haynes explained his debt to Bowie: "There are all of these languages that keep people in place that conform us to a sort of set of terms. It's why I think the whole idea of identity…as something that is somewhat of a straitjacket." In Haynes's view, Bowie and glam rock blew the doors off standard notions of identity. Constructing a sense of self, Haynes said, is "a struggle for stability or some sense of normalcy…. All of the sudden, these teenage kids—who are in a constant state of instability, uncertainty—have this image of a bisexual space alien up onstage." The Bowie-led explosion of what it meant to be young and alive in the '70s is crystallized in *Velvet Goldmine* when a gay kid sees a glammed-up Rhys Meyers at a press conference and imagines it helping him come out to his parents.

Haynes says his films are all about the "little accidents" of safe space where his characters can enjoy freedom outside the constraints of an uptight society. But glam rock and Bowie, he says, were "a big accident" that opened up a whole new world and continues to widen our perception of what it means to be cool, accepted, and loved. □

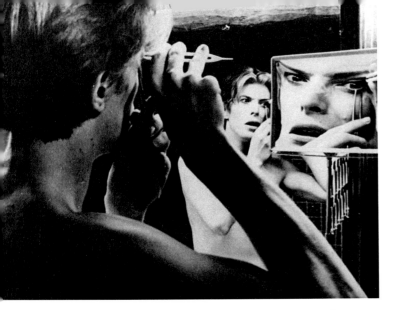

SECRET VISITOR

How, for one novelist, THE MAN WHO
FELL TO EARTH *cast its spell.*

› **WORDS** *by* **JONATHAN LETHEM**
ORIGINALLY PUBLISHED IN
THE NEW YORKER, FEBRUARY 28, 2005

My mother and her boyfriend took me to a midday showing of *The Man Who Fell to Earth* at the Quad Cinema on West 13th Street in Manhattan. *The Man Who Fell to Earth* stars David Bowie as a gentle and moody alien visitor to our planet, one who, upon encountering man's inhumanity to alien, becomes increasingly bitter and self-abnegating, until he ends up a decadent and drunken pop star. This was the bowdlerized American release, missing the blatant sex scenes that have since been restored, though David Bowie's attempt to present his "true self" to his human lover, played by Candy Clark—shedding his disguise, he reveals goatlike slit pupils, and a smooth, doll-like bump in place of his genitals—was shocking to me.

As we three stepped back out into the daylight of Manhattan, I was deeply immersed in the spell of the film. I'd been reading Ray Bradbury's *Martian Chronicles* and a handful of other classic science-fiction stories, and *alien equals alienated* was a rebus I grasped. Any one of these people I see walking around me, I remember thinking, in astonishment, as we made our way back to the subway, could be like him. By "like him" I meant, or thought I meant: a secret visitor from another planet. But my wonder at the film was really wonder at the force of my identification with the figure of the misunderstood alien. I didn't for a minute imagine that I wasn't an earthling, so what I really meant was: Any one of these people I see walking around me could be like me. Could feel like me, just as I felt like Bowie. That is to say, subjective, sad, and special. □

▸ *continued from previous page* fact—and of the closing shot, with Newton quietly stranded, in a broad-brimmed hat, at a café table—has swelled since the film's release. It compounds the myth of Bowie: not so much a permanent resident on planet Earth as a baffled yet well-intentioned visitor, who urges us to take a step sideways, inspect our regular habits, and see them for the peculiarities they are. I get all that, and its appeal is hard to resist, just as the call of infinite space was to Major Tom, but equally I am convinced by Bowie's mild protestations, in a BBC interview of 2002: "I wouldn't dream of getting on a spaceship. It would scare the shit out of me," he said. "I'm scared going down to the end of the garden."

One thing to be wary of, with Bowie as with the Beatles, is the grave danger of forgetting how funny he was, and how easily amused. Mingled with the freak show was a generous stock of common sense, plus a measure of companionable cheer, and that Martian glare was readily supplanted by a grin. Behind him stood the music hall, and the garrulous double-act of Peter Cook and Dudley Moore, and other staples of popular diversion; one band he joined in the '60s, the Lower Third, used to perform "Chim Chim Cher-ee," from *Mary Poppins,* and "Modern Love" is not so modern that it can't afford to glance back, in the exhortation "Get me to the church on time," to *My Fair Lady.* The octave between the two syllables of "Starman," in Bowie's song of that name, is lifted from the interval between "Some" and "where" in "Somewhere Over the Rainbow." On a chat show, Bowie spoke warmly of his radio days, as

OTHERWORLDLY
The man who had a novelty hit with the single "The Laughing Gnome" in 1967 became, nearly 20 years later, the king of the goblins in *Labyrinth;* pausing to reflect in *The Man Who Fell to Earth* (above, left).

song when it appeared in *Jack Reacher* or last year's *Aloha*. But hear it again, and afresh, as it accompanies the closing credits of *Dogville* (2003) and *Manderlay* (2005). The director, in both cases, was Lars von Trier, and he overlays the music with a scalding montage of photographs: first, of Depression-era poverty and alcoholism, and second, of African-Americans not just shunted to the margins of society but openly harassed and hanged. The song continues to chivvy you along (Luther Vandross had a hand in the backing vocals), but, thanks to the images, you are returned, as the casual listener might not be, to the pity and the scorn of Bowie's words:

> All the way from Washington
> Her breadwinner begs off the bathroom floor
> We live for just these 20 years
> Do we have to die for the 50 more?

The lyrical drive was no less strong in "Cat People (Putting out Fire)," which, for Bowie admirers who like to track their ▸ *continued on page 109*

a child—hearing his mother sing along to "Oh for the Wings of a Dove," and picking up on the darting melody of, wait for it, "Tubby the Tuba."

In short, like most deities, he was never quite as solemn as his worshippers. To read some of the more breathless elegies, you might think that Bowie's adoption of multiple personalities arose from a genuine psychological crack. Doubtless, he could feel as lost and as unmoored as the rest of us, especially in our youth, and his music famously gave succor to those who believed themselves to be adrift or misunderstood. That is something to be grateful for, yet still, to cleave to a work of art, in any medium, because of its therapeutic benefits is to risk neglecting the artist's sense of play. His or her right to fool around, and to happen upon beauty in the fooling, matters just as much—I hate to say it—as the rescue of your soul. That is another reason to relish Bowie's involvement with the movies, even if it amounted to little more than a flirtation; it reinforced the ludic aspect of Bowie, who had, at other times, been lured into the apocalyptic mode. His most enjoyable turn could well be as Andy Warhol, in *Basquiat* (1996), where he got everything right—the prim shuffle of the walk, and the vaporous drone of the ruminations. Bowie was at ease, playing the part of a guy who played the part of himself. Nothing was not a game.

If you abstracted Bowie the actor from our screens, he would still haunt the senses of cinema-goers, because his music has crept into movies, sometimes when you expect it least. It was right and proper, for instance, that John Hughes—much of whose work, so goofy at first blush, seems riper and sadder with the years—should have feted the characters of *Sixteen Candles* (1984) with a blast of Bowie's "Young Americans." Molly Ringwald, for one, deserves no less. You will have brushed past the same

"I'M NOT A GOOD FINGER WAGGER. I'M NOT A GOOD MORALIST."

NO TURNING BACK
Bowie in London
in 1990.

**PHOTOGRAPH BY
CLIVE ARROWSMITH**

FRAME BY FRAME

From his EXPERIMENTAL *efforts in the late*
'60s to his recent SWAN SONG, *Bowie has few rivals*
for the title KING OF THE MUSIC VIDEO.

› **WORDS** *by* **PHILIP SHERBURNE**
ORIGINALLY PUBLISHED ON PITCHFORK.COM, JANUARY 13, 2016

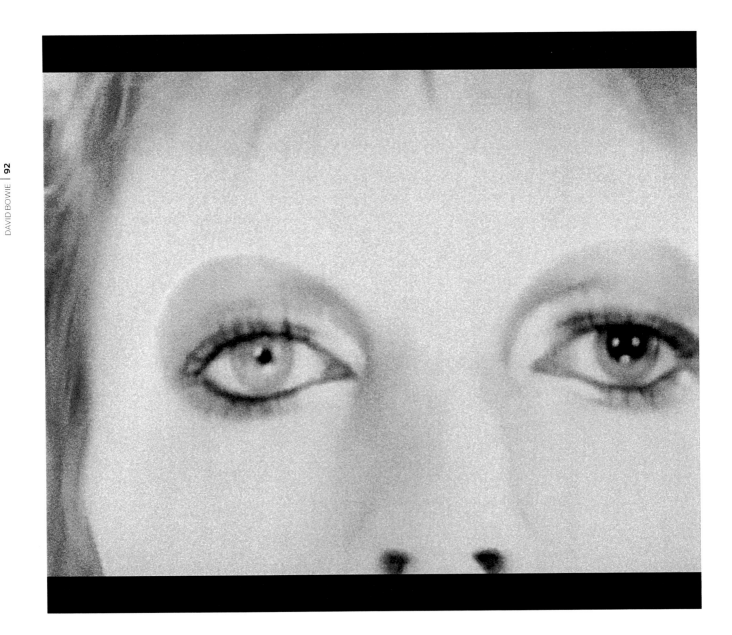

No musician understood the power of the image—still, moving, mime, puppets, you name it—better than David Bowie. He was making music videos before MTV would eventually consecrate the form; and it could be argued his emphasis on character, costume, narrative, and personal reinvention helped set the stage for the arrival of music videos as a crucial artistic medium.

His "Life on Mars?" (1973) established Bowie as a man in control of spectacle. There's nothing to see here but Bowie himself. His expression and body language are as rich as any widescreen epic: those blue-shadowed eyes, bobbing in the washed-out frame; the gravity-defying fluff of his hairdo; the perfect curl of his lips in profile. Of all the images that presented Bowie as a man from outer space, the opening shot of "'Heroes'" (1977), with the singer similarly wreathed in luminous fog, head tipped slightly to one side, is one of the most elegant. As the camera slowly zooms in on his elven features, he really does look like a creature from another world, at once intimate and strange. In "D.J." (1979), there's no fancy concept, no special effects—except for a couple of minor explosions— just Bowie wreaking havoc in a radio station's D.J. booth, getting kissed by passersby on the street, and looking absolutely ravishing in a pink belted jumpsuit and gas mask.

He embraced striking and indelible images like these in the '80s. "Ashes to Ashes" (1980) ushered in the new decade in fine, outré fashion with Martian landscapes, padded walls, a bulldozer, and Bowie in a creepy Pierrot costume. In "Fashion" (1980), Bowie and his band play for an indifferent nightclub audience—Bowie dancing like a gerbil and making truly awful cocaine faces—intercut with images of wildly costumed fashionistas waiting in soup lines. At 1:35, his dancers convulse wildly, a move that he'll reprise, to terrifying effect, in "Blackstar."

This creative vitality fueled a symbiotic relationship with MTV and catapulted him to new levels of worldwide fame. But that didn't stop him from criticizing the company: He famously chided the V.J. Mark Goodman in an interview because of the network's reluctance to air videos by black artists. Meanwhile, Bowie continued to use his videos as an opportunity to develop his radical gender-fluidity, and make pointed critiques of racial and class injustice.

His collaboration with Queen, "Under Pressure" (1981), juxtaposed clips of old films, like the German expressionist *Nosferatu*, with footage of city crowds, imploding buildings, violent demonstrations, and outdoor rock festivals. "China Girl" presented a critique of Orientalism as Orientalism itself. The thing Bowie does with the corners of his eyes can be difficult to watch, and it's even more difficult to watch the fake execution of his female lead. But you've got to respect his determination to make the viewer squirm.

And then, at the end of his life, Bowie created some of the most triumphant work of his entire career, turning his imminent death into three very different, and profoundly moving, video treatments. "The Stars (Are Out Tonight)" (2013) brought Bowie together with Tilda Swinton (at last) alongside an assortment of incubi and succubi in an eerie satire of celebrity. With "Blackstar" (2015) Bowie seemed to be art-directing his ascension to the heavens. Amid fallen spacesuits, bejeweled skulls, strange rituals, convulsive dancers, a girl with a tail, and a total eclipse, Bowie—bandaged and with buttons for eyes—faces down the infinite.

Bowie's final video, "Lazarus" (2016) is hard to watch. Not because he looks ill—he comes across as vital as he'd ever been. (Just look at him in that woolen jumpsuit, busting out Bob Fosse moves.) But beneath the surface is something resembling terror. As he scribbles away with an old-fashioned ink pen, he bites his nails, then grimaces comically. He looks afraid, but also eager to get it all over with, to finally be free. Everybody knows him now, it's true, but as he pulls back into his closet, it's impossible not to feel like he's still one step ahead of us all. □

APT PUPILS
In the clips for "Life on Mars?" from 1973 (left) and "Lazarus," from 2016, it's all in the eyes.

THE SPIRIT OF '77
Recording *"Heroes"* with guitarist Robert Fripp (far left), producer Tony Visconti, and Brian Eno at Berlin's Hansa Tonstudio.

10 ESSENTIAL SONGS

BOWIE *released dozens of* SINGLES *during a decades-long career that found him infatuated with everything from* STARRY-EYED *space-folk to* GUITAR-HERO *glam rock to gurgling electronica. Reducing that output to a single* BEST-OF *list is impossible, but here are the tunes that display* HIS VERVE, HIS VIGOR, *and his ongoing love of the new.*

› **WORDS** *by* **BRIAN RAFTERY**
ORIGINALLY PUBLISHED ON WIRED.COM, JANUARY 11, 2016

1. " 'HEROES' "
"Heroes" *(1977)*
Bowie had just hit 30 when this was released—old enough to know heartache and defeat, but young enough to still be hopeful. The result is a gorgeously beguiling space-opera love song, a wall of swan-diving syn-thesizers, gut-wrung vocals, and Cold War heat.

2. "CHANGES"
(with Alicia Keys at the Black Ball fundraiser, 2006)
This is Bowie, in his last public performance, playing the 1971 song that, eons from now, will still be one of his most-quoted, most-karaoked, most-ch-ch-ch-ch-cherished. Has any song so perfectly (and maybe inadvertently) encapsulated its per-former—his outlook, his ethos, his appeal?

3. "BLACKSTAR"
Blackstar *(2016)*
The opening track of Bowie's final album is a 10-minute rumination about death and iden-tity that could have felt like a pre-emptive self-eulogy. But listen to this intricate opus and ask yourself: What other 60-something musician could have journeyed so far into himself and re-turned with something this gorgeously spacey and affecting?

4. "SUFFRAGETTE CITY"
The Rise and Fall of Ziggy Stardust and the Spiders from Mars *(1972)*
A pure sex tempest of Little Richard boogie-woogie, glam-rock riffage, and schoolboy hormones. "Suffragette City" had one of the de-liciously weirdest trajec-tories in pop-culture his-tory: A horndog anthem by a bisexual alien that would end up an unlikely gym-jam for classic-rock-lovin' dads. Outta sight.

5. "YOUNG AMERICANS"
Young Americans *(1975)*
Ain't there one damn song that can make you break down and cry?

6. "UNDER PRESSURE"
(isolated vocal version, 1981)
This long-circulated al-ternate version of Bowie's hit with Queen—which strips out every element save for Bowie and Fred-die Mercury's vocals—is a reminder of how beauti-fully supernatural Bow-ie's voice could be.

7. "STRANGERS WHEN WE MEET"
Outside *(1995)*
Bowie's catalog was er-ratic in the '90s, but there

are plenty of worthy entries for those willing to dig around, from the paranoid tech-scuzz of "I'm Afraid of Americans" to the messy grandeur of "Little Wonder." This straightforward (for Bowie) tale of old friends and fading memories was one of the loveliest of his career.

8. "MODERN LOVE"
Let's Dance *(1983)*
Is there any way to get across just how ecstatic and life-conquering Bowie's 1983 hit can make you feel? There is not. Luckily, though, the scene of Greta Gerwig sprinting through the streets of Manhattan in *Frances Ha* while "Modern Love" plays comes pretty close.

9. "GOLDEN YEARS"
Station to Station *(1975)*
This is your Bowie on drugs: It sounds like the work of a man in love with a half-dozen musical styles at once, but unwilling to settle down with any one of them. "Golden Years" is a future-thinking throwback that was funky enough to earn Bowie a spot on *Soul Train*.

10. "LIFE ON MARS?"
Hunky Dory *(1971)*
This didn't become a hit until two years after the album, but "Life on Mars?" remains the most quintessentially Bowie-ish song of his early career: A weirdo rallying cry gussied up as a cabaret number, with lyrics so alien and disorienting, listeners still puzzle over them today ("It's on America's tortured brow / That Mickey Mouse has grown up a cow"). □

10 BEST ALBUMS
Having recorded more than TWO DOZEN *studio efforts, Bowie always looked at the* LP *as one cohesive* WORK OF ART. *Here is a chronology of the greats.*

› **WORDS** *b y* **ROB TANNENBAUM**

HUNKY DORY *(1971)*
In the '60s, Bowie miscast himself as a hippie, which you can still hear in his fourth album's artisanal, whole-grain production. "Changes," often interpreted as an autobiographical song, and "Oh! You Pretty Things" are his first great defenses of youth culture. "Kooks" is one of the warmest, most honest songs ever written by a father to a baby. *Hunky Dory* is memorable and smart, but not quite daring. **Don't overlook:** "Queen Bitch"

THE RISE AND FALL OF ZIGGY STARDUST AND THE SPIDERS FROM MARS *(1972)*
Bowie organized his gift for concept, drama, and catchy anthems into this story of a fictional rock band led by a sexy, charismatic singer who might be an alien. The Ziggy image followed him for years, and invented an ongoing tradition of rock singers creating personas and mythologies. This is his strongest collection of songs, as opposed to experiments or tricks. **Don't overlook:** "Moonage Daydream"

ALADDIN SANE *(1973)*
After years of struggle, Bowie was a star. He didn't entirely settle onto a throne. "Play that avant-garde stuff," he instructed Mike Garson, who added a famously digressive piano solo to the title song. Bowie salts these crude, riff-based songs with tilted musical touches, and sings about revolution, rent boys, fame, suicide, and the dystopia he saw while traversing Nixon's America. **Don't overlook:** "Panic in Detroit"

YOUNG AMERICANS *(1975)*
Bowie cheekily referred to his ninth album

as "plastic soul," because he recorded it mostly in Philadelphia, with funk and R&B musicians (plus John Lennon, who co-wrote and sang on the hit single "Fame"). But Bowie's lyrics have never been less mysterious: The title song acutely describes a woman desperate for love and disappointed by sex. **Don't overlook:** "Fascination"

STATION TO STATION *(1976)*
There's still some funk in "Golden Years," his third U.S. Top 20 hit, but Bowie was turning to the clipped, robotic music of two German bands, Neu! and Kraftwerk. In "TVC15," his girlfriend crawls inside a television set, and elsewhere his lyrics are full of panic: "Run for the shadows," "Who ▸ *continued on page 108*

"I STOPPED BEING AN OUTSIDER QUITE SOME TIME AGO. IT'S THAT I'VE JUST GOT TO CONVINCE THE REST OF THE WORLD THAT I'VE STOPPED BEING THE OUTSIDER THEY THOUGHT I WAS."

A VISION IN WHITE
Bowie cuts a striking figure in one of his final photo shoots, to promote the release of *Blackstar*.

ASHES TO ASHES

After a lifetime of shifting IDENTITIES, Bowie found
a way to mean something to almost everyone, inspiring an audience
as DIVERSE AND CURIOUS as his own
work. Those touched by his art REMEMBER the man.

› **PHOTOGRAPH** *by* **SNOWDON**

"I'm happy. Hope you're happy, too. / I've loved. All I've needed: love."

STATUESQUE
Bowie puts himself
on a pedestal for
Vogue U.K. in 1978.

STRIKING A CORD
The Thin White Duke
performs during
the Station to Station
tour in 1976.

A NATURAL COLLABORATOR

› **WORDS** *by*
HILTON ALS

NEWYORKER.COM, JANUARY 11, 2016

This was not supposed to happen. Ever. Because he had been so many people over the course of his grand and immense career, it was inconceivable that he wouldn't continue to be many people—a myriad of folks in a beautiful body who would reflect times to come, times none of us could imagine but that he could. He always got to the unknown first.

David Robert Jones was born, in Brixton, to working-class parents, on January 8, 1947, and the Brixton of his day was a changing place—home to members of the "Windrush generation," West Indians who, like immigrants everywhere, had come to England looking for a better way. And the music those islanders brought to their new island no doubt influenced the artist who always wanted to be an artist; indeed, Bowie's need to perform—to be recognized as different—made itself known when he was a child. In movement class, he claimed center stage, striking attitudes that his instructors found unusual, original. He was always an original, not least because he defied "Englishness"—not making a fuss, not standing out—by making theatre out of his body and that incredible face.

Everyone knows the story. Jones—who did not shrink from a fight—was arguing with a friend over a girl when his friend punched him in one of his blue eyes; somehow, his fingernail got caught in Bowie's left eye. The result was a permanently dilated pupil. Just as Marlon Brando broke his nose while horsing around backstage during the Broadway run of *A Streetcar Named Desire* and the accident added to, rather than detracted from, his beauty, Bowie's infirmity only added to his allure, an "oddity" whose romanticism imagined other places in addition to this world—places he invented and filled with longing.

A natural collaborator, Bowie used his considerable fame to help popularize artists who would have had less of a chance without him. Nothing's better than watching Bowie play keyboards for Dinah Shore on her TV show in 1977. He was there to support an artist he loved—Iggy Pop, whose seminal, first solo album, *The Idiot*, had come out that year. In an interview on MTV, recorded in 1990, Pop talked about how Bowie had rescued him, basically, from being a street person, and helped him to become an artist. On the Shore show, Pop's outrageous body gyrates, twists, and turns as he sings "Sister Midnight"; at one point you can hear Bowie laughing at all the antics. Bowie then sits down with Shore, she of genteel 1940s movie musicals, and attempts to explain, with great seriousness and in depth, why Pop was important, and why their collaboration worked.

Rock stars are not generally known for their generosity to other artists; it takes a lot to get up there and be such a huge presence. Early on, Bowie realized he was more himself—had more of himself—when he built bridges between different worlds. I wonder how much of that he owed to what he saw in Brixton. Two years before he worked with Pop, Bowie made his first masterpiece—1975's *Young Americans*. Bowie called it "plastic soul," which was an honest thought. Bowie was not a soul man; he was borrowing from soul artists his new self, backed by incredible black artists like Ava Cherry and Luther Vandross. Dressed in high-waisted pants and carrying a cane, Bowie's elegance and showmanship on *The Dick Cavett Show*, in 1974, while he was getting his plastic-soul thing together, didn't so much diminish the rather square-looking Cavett as inject a powerful social formula: what blackness looked like on a white artist.

Bowie was a miscegenationist at a time when it wasn't necessarily cool, or tolerated. Bowie was "queer" in that way, and things only got queerer on the Cavett show when Bowie introduced Cherry, his lover at the time, to the audience. There, again, he was framing a performer he liked by conferring some of his star power on her. (Bowie worked on Cherry's album *People from Bad Homes*. Check it out. Her sound is not as big as Betty Davis's, but there are loads of wonderful moments on it, including the lead track, written by Bowie.) Halfway through "Foot Stompin'," on the Cavett show, Bowie points to Cherry, the blond-haired black woman to his left, and says, "Cherry!" She dances a bit, and the moment is gone, but not the memory of Bowie watching his friend perform in the aura of his generosity.

Indeed, Bowie's rendition of "Foot Stompin'" was the artist's tribute to the Flares, a doo-wop group that recorded in the 1950s and early '60s. Back then, a young David Robert Jones thrilled to the records his father brought home, including those made by that outrageous, vulnerable showman Little Richard. When he heard "Tutti Frutti," Bowie said once, he knew he'd heard God. Little Richard's uncommon look and feeling were a part of what he meant to project in this common

world. Bowie, too. He was an Englishman who was sometimes afraid of Americans and fame but, on his final record, could sing "Look at me / I'm in heaven" as a way of describing where he wanted to end up, maybe, but definitely when Bowie—the outsider who made different kids feel like dancing in that difference, and who had a genius for friendship, too—had lived since we knew him. □

*Hilton Als, **The New Yorker**'s theater critic, has been a staff writer since 1994.*

IN MEMORY OF MY GREAT GAY SAINT

› **WORDS** *by*
ALEX FRANK

PITCHFORK.COM, JANUARY 11, 2016

If gayness were a church, I'd say we make Bowie one of its anointed saints. I cannot quantify precisely the effect he has had on the increasing visibility of gay and trans peoples throughout the world, but there are few pop culture figures I'd give more credit to for expanding the boundaries of what we think of as beautiful. Bowie wasn't exactly "gay" himself—he ultimately married and had children with women—but he did stoke the flames of queer rumors long before it was fashionable to do so, telling *Playboy* in 1976 that he was bisexual, while in the same breath admitting that his sexual fluidity was something of a publicity stunt. "I just got my leg over a lot," he told British talk show host Jonathan Ross with a laugh and a smile in 2002 when asked about his youthful relationships with men.

For so many gay men, the first pangs of childhood shame have actually nothing to do with an attraction to other boys and everything to do with the emergence of certain traits often described as "feminine." Not all gay men are "girly," that's true. But I was. I remember drawing on my hand with pastel bubbly pens before a particularly joyless middle school Latin teacher pulled me aside and ordered me to wash it off, telling me that's something that only girls do. I scrubbed my skin so furiously with hot water that it hurt.

When I discovered Bowie a little later in high school, he was the first person I can recall doing the opposite of what that teacher did: He made being a girly boy seem not just brave, but cool. Through my sadness, I keep remembering that he does not have to be alive for some fresh new 16-year-old boy—or girl, or girl wanting to be a boy, or boy wanting to be a girl, or some person who has no gender at all—to discover Bowie, and help remind whomever needs it that not so long after that part of queer life that seems like hell, it will feel like heaven. □

Alex Frank is a freelance writer and editor.

COSMIC SALUTATIONS

› **WORDS** *by*
JAMES WOLCOTT
VANITYFAIR.COM, JANUARY 12, 2016

The paramount concert performance of Bowie I saw was his Madison Square Garden appearance for *Station to Station*, the stage illuminated by long white tubes of light that evoked an industrial site and punctuated the numbers with spaceship flashes. It was Bowie breaking into dance after the song's long, ticktock-train-station intro that I most remember, and when I look at other performances of the title track, I marvel at how beautifully, elegantly Bowie moved onstage and in videos. It wasn't the herky-jerky mugging of Mick Jagger or the heavy shouldering of Bruce Springsteen, but something far more air-slicing and Zen succinct; his gestures were like cosmic salutations. Otherworldly and extra-dimensional, both astronaut and android, ancient and ageless, he seemed to have been sent to us to induct us into new modes of dream-walking. None of that Morrissey morbidity about him. Even during the thick, glum Cold War worst of the '70s and the early '80s, the sonic postcards of Bowie's Berlin trilogy (*Low, "Heroes," The Lodger*) were antidotes to nihilism and nostalgia. What a run Bowie had in the '70s, and the remarkable thing is that in the decades to follow, he never became a caricature of himself, a museum collectible. The critic Marvin Mudrick once said that we should never downplay what artists have given us and try to reduce them to our level by saying they're people just like us, because they're *not*. Their genius is on a whole higher plane. The outpouring of grief over the death of David Bowie is proof that we never truly cherish how much that art and pleasure have meant to us until the being who gave it to us has been taken away. □

James Wolcott writes for **Vanity Fair.**

NO MORE *NEXT DAY*

› **WORDS** *by*
DAVID KAMP
VANITYFAIR.COM, JANUARY 11, 2016

Did any musician of the rock era more effectively bridge *outré* experimentalism and pop appeal? I can't think of one. My favorite Bowie single is 1980's "Ashes to Ashes," the zoinked-out sequel to "Space Oddity" ("We know Major Tom's a junkie"), which is so layered with ideas, effects, and stuff—catchy Buddy Holly–

style verses; flanged, melty piano; interior-monologue babble; Anthony Newley–esque crooning—that one can never grow sick of hearing it. Speaking more eloquently to this point, R.E.M.'s Michael Stipe once said of "Ashes to Ashes," "It's so audacious as a piece of writing. You can go into any bar in the world, and if they play that song, watch people around the room. Each will sing along to a separate part. There's about seven parts people sing along to. It's the audacity of not only writing about Major Tom, but then making it this flawless mess." □

David Kamp has been a **Vanity Fair** *contributing editor since 1996.*

A PERFECT EXIT

› **WORDS** *by*
BRUCE HANDY
VANITYFAIR.COM, JANUARY 11, 2016

What timing. Has any performer ever made as impeccable an exit as David Bowie did? He released a terrific new album on a Friday, as ambitious as any in his career, and then died the following Sunday, after what has been reported as a year-and-a-half struggle with cancer. This is probably not the moment to be weighing showbiz imperatives, but I can't help but think that Bowie just one-upped Beyoncé and Kendrick Lamar and their surprise album drops. Talk about dropping the mic. Is that callous? Surely Bowie, as theatrical a performer as rock and pop have produced, must have appreciated his own *coup de théâtre*, whether intentional or not.

Like all of Bowie's best music, *Blackstar* takes multiple hearings to begin to reveal itself, and I can't say I have a handle on it yet. (Not that one ever has a "handle" on art, but you know what I mean.) His death obviously adds poignancy and new meaning to the album. Was it intended as a last testament, a parting gift, a candle lit against the darkness? It's hard not to hear it that way, at least today. As Bowie sings on the title song:

Something happened on the day he died
Spirit rose a meter and stepped aside
Somebody else took his place and bravely cried
(I'm a blackstar, I'm a star's star, I'm a blackstar)

On the record's final track, "I Can't Give Everything Away," Bowie croons that phrase with a long, pregnant pause between "everything" and "away," the second word buoyed by a lovely, bittersweet harmony—Bowie's voice multi-tracked, I think. At song's end, the final "away" drifts off into an initially turbulent, then oceanic, and finally serene soundscape.

"Achingly beautiful" is one of the worst critical clichés, right up there with "fiercely intelligent"—but here it's apt. The song sure sounds like a farewell. □
Bruce Handy first joined **Vanity Fair** *as a senior articles editor in 1999.*

DISCOVERING HIS WORLD

› **WORDS** *by*
SARAH LARSON
NEWYORKER.COM, JANUARY 11, 2016

For so many people, loving David Bowie was an integral part of growing up. I discovered him in fourth grade, when the album *Let's Dance* came out, with "Modern Love" and other delights (that glorious pop assertiveness, yellow suit, yellow hair), and further in sixth, when "Blue Jean," from *Tonight* (police bike, turned-up nose), thrilled me. This morning, in one of my Bowie commiserations, a longtime close friend said that she could imagine whole worlds around each of his songs, because Bowie's lyrics were so visual and narrative. I suddenly remembered that in seventh grade she'd had a vivid nightmare about "Cat People." I explored backward in Bowie's catalogue as I grew into being ready for it. Discovering his world, that richly strange visual and narrative world, meant entering a more adult one. □
Sarah Larson is a cultural correspondent for newyorker.com.

HUNTER AND HIS GAME

› **WORDS** *by*
COREY SEYMOUR
VOGUE.COM, JANUARY 11, 2016

From the first time I heard him to the last, Bowie was always relevant to my life, always relevant to the world we lived in. I never met the man and had only one "encounter," though even that might be overstating the case. In 1992 I was working at *Rolling Stone*, which was celebrating its 25th anniversary with a big party at the Four Seasons. My responsibility that night was to make sure that Hunter S. Thompson arrived with his speech written; when he arrived without said speech, I was to keep the throngs of fans and celebrity friends away from him while he wrote it at the bar—something he actually, shockingly, did. Then we were given the nod—Hunter was up next. We slowly made our way through the crowd and into the Pool Room and edged our way right up below the dais—directly in front of David Bowie, who was seated with Iman at a front row table. Ed Bradley was beginning to introduce Hunter when suddenly Hunter dropped down to the ground and sat, cross-legged, directly in front of Bowie, and produced a large canister of cocaine from his sock. Then he began to snort it with a hollowed-out plastic Bic pen, rather loudly. Almost instantly, Hunter rapped me—hard—on my shin and whisper-barked, "Shield me, goddammit!" I did as I was told, but I couldn't help but notice that as I did, the shin just a few inches to the left of my head was David Bowie's. I looked up and caught Bowie's eye for a long moment, and I'll never forget his expression—at once bewildered, amused, and detached, with this thin-lipped, straight-line smile and slightly raised eyebrows. It meant nothing; it meant everything. □
Corey Seymour is a senior editor at **Vogue**.

MOURNING MR. BOWIE

› **WORDS** *by*
JULIA FELSENTHAL
VOGUE.COM, JANUARY 11, 2016

He always kept his mystery about him, even when he was on his way out," said Gabrielle, one of many fans who had by midmorning begun to gather outside the building where David Bowie and his wife, Iman, sometimes lived, on Lafayette Street in Soho. Gabrielle, a chiropractor who works in the music industry, said she actually adjusted Bowie's back a few times, though the last time was about two decades ago and she doesn't remember much. "I think he was a very shy person," she said. "But I didn't know him well."

In an age when broadcasting one's health struggles has become de rigueur, Bowie chose to do the opposite. Ever enigmatic, ever sly, he slipped away from this world with stealthy, catlike grace.

Across the street, a mound of bouquets was beginning to accumulate on the sidewalk. There were candles burning in bell jars; flickering out of wabi-sabi ceramic vessels; and one tall votive, encased in a glass tube festooned with Christian iconography. Mourners trickled by, braving freezing temperatures, made timid by the overwhelming presence of media, reporters scribbling descriptions of the scene, photographers jockeying for position, producers cruising for interview subjects. One grinning reporter had his iPhone poking out of his shirt's front chest pocket, volume pumped up, the tinny blare of "Starman" just audible. "It's too quiet," he said later, when his phone died. He left to recharge the battery…. □
Julia Felsenthal is a senior culture writer at vogue.com.

ANTHEMS FOR
THE MOON

▶ *continued from page 25*

most indelible conceits: a tattooed man who lets strange tales play out like hypnotic films within the confines of his writhing body art.

Also in 1967, Bowie's "We Are Hungry Men" sketched a nightmare scenario in which a messianic leader devises a new solution to world hunger, a proposal that's rendered irrelevant, in a *Twilight Zone*–like twist, when the starving mob opts instead for cannibalism. One year before the release of "We Are Hungry Men," the author Harry Harrison published *Make Room! Make Room!*, a grim novel with a strikingly similar concept that would eventually become the source material for the 1973 movie *Soylent Green*.

Bowie's alignment with the sci-fi and fantasy zeitgeist didn't end there. His 1969 song "Cygnet Committee" mixed gentle acoustic guitars with a lurching, elaborate arrangement, and a plot involving a cultural revolution gone wrong. It foretold not only the imminent demise of hippie utopianism, but the apocalyptic atmosphere—or lack of atmosphere—of Bowie's cosmic work to come.

In a short film for "Space Oddity" made in 1969, Bowie's face is cold, serene, composed. Unlike the bulky spacesuits in the widely publicized photos of the ongoing Apollo space missions, however, his uniform is sleek, form-fitting chrome that enhances rather than obscures his lithe physique. There's an air of extravagant vanity to this particular space explorer, as well as one of aloofness. His helmet secure, he steps outside his space capsule. The void beckons, a womb of oblivion that threatens to swallow our hero.

The "Space Oddity" clip followed Stanley Kubrick's groundbreaking 1968 film *2001: A Space Odyssey*, and the similarity between "Space Oddity" and *A Space Odyssey* are entirely intentional; Bowie, who worked in marketing in his youth, knew the power of synergy. In *2001*—which was based on the 1951 short story "The Sentinel" by Arthur

C. Clarke—astronauts are forced to confront both the travails of artificial intelligence gone awry and the devastating metaphysical awe of discovering alien life.

There are no aliens in "Space Oddity"— those beings would factor greatly in some of Bowie's best-known work to come—but a devastating metaphysical awe underpins the song. Faced with the vastness of the cosmos, Major Tom laments in newfound futility, "Planet Earth is blue, and there's nothing I can do." That ennui, bordering on paralysis, humanized astronauts in a way that NASA's heroic sloganeering failed to do. As Bowie has noted, "The publicity image of the spaceman at work is of an automaton rather than a human being, and my Major Tom is nothing if not a human being."

There was another work of science fiction that informed "Space Oddity." After having drawn on Bradbury's *The Illustrated Man* for the song "Karma Man," Bowie took inspiration from Bradbury's story "Kaleidoscope," which described a group of astronauts falling to their fiery deaths through the cosmos after their rocket explodes. "I'm stepping through the door," Bowie sings from the perspective of Major Tom. "And I'm floating in a most peculiar way / And the stars look very different today." Those lines would eventually gain a profound secondary connotation: Bowie himself was the rock star who was looking very different, a striking evolution that would continue over the next few years.

"I want it to be the first anthem of the moon," Bowie once said of "Space Oddity," adding drolly, "I suppose it's an antidote to space fever, really." And the BBC did play the song during its live coverage of the moon landing. But by the mid-'70s, space fever had cooled, just as disillusionment with many of the achievements of the '60s had set in.

In 1973 Bowie gloomily predicted, "This is a mad planet. It's doomed to madness." So, in a sense, he left it behind. Following in his creation's footsteps, he became an explorer throughout the '70s, with each album offering a dispatch from an uncharted planet.

With its trippy chants and repetitive chords, his 1970 single "Memory of a Free Festival" seems, at first listen, to lapse back into peace-and-love idealism. But Bowie spikes it with science fiction, singing, "We scanned the skies with rainbow eyes and saw machines of every shape and size." Those machines being extraterrestrial spacecraft, a phenomenon that is brought into sharper focus in the next line: "We talked with tall Venusians passing through." There's no hint of novelty to the song; it's the sound of Bowie

fully buying into his own alternatingly euphoric and apocalyptic fantasies.

"Memory of a Free Festival" featured guitarist Mick Ronson, who, along with drummer Woody Woodmansey and bassist Trevor Bolder, would make up the Spiders From Mars, the backing band for Ziggy Stardust in Bowie's band-within-a-band spectacle. It's also one of the few points in time that could be considered to be the genesis of glam rock.

Injecting a dizzying dose of color, decadence, and fantasy to a rock culture that had begun to emphasize the music's more earthy qualities, glam came more fully into fruition on Bowie's 1970 album, *The Man Who Sold the World*. In another echo of *2001*, the song "Saviour Machine" puts forth a frightening future in which an advanced supercomputer, like Clarke and Kubrick's HAL 9000, begins to toy with the humans that it was built to serve.

Bowie dug deeper into his science-fiction background on *Hunky Dory*. The 1971 album employs the term "Homo superior" as a descriptor of the next stage of human evolution beyond mere Homo sapiens—a science-fiction trope that dates back at least to Olaf Stapledon's influential 1935 novel *Odd John*, which posits the conflict between people with extraordinary mental powers and the human society to which they've been born. By the early '70s, the concept had trickled all the way down to the mutants of Marvel's *X-Men* comics, but Bowie took it in a more chilling direction—that is, toward Friedrich Nietzsche's notion of the *Übermensch*, or superman, a theme he established more overtly on the track "The Supermen" from *The Man Who Sold the World*.

A flash of the old space explorer surfaces on "Life on Mars?" which came the same year as the launch of Russia's Mars probes as well as the U.S. launch of the Mars-bound Mariner 9. Mars was in the air, although for a boy who was enthralled by Gustav Holst's "Mars" theme from *The Planets*—not to mention another of Ray Bradbury's masterworks, 1950's *The Martian Chronicles*—it was inevitable that Bowie would add the Red Planet to his ever-expanding cosmology-in-song.

"Life on Mars?" uses the red planet as a symbol for alienation, social estrangement, and cultural decline, with Bowie once again playing an aloof, dispassionate observer of the human race. For Bowie, glam rock's co-opting of science fiction was a way to express the otherness and isolation he had felt since a child, feelings that drew him to the pages of science fiction in the first place. He also went so far as to describe another *Hunky Dory* song, "The Bewlay Brothers," as "*Star Trek* in a leather jacket."

That tension between engagement and escapism hit its peak in 1972 with the release of *The Rise and Fall of Ziggy Stardust and the Spiders from Mars*. A concept album about, according to Bowie, a "Martian messiah who twanged a guitar," the record wends its way through a Burroughsian apocalypse just a half a decade away. The opening song, "Five Years," isn't really about 1977; it's about the point on the horizon in which the future perpetually splinters into an infinite web of maybe. That uncertain tomorrow is personified in "Starman," a first-contact scenario involving an alien—Ziggy Stardust himself—who would "like to come and meet us but he thinks he'd blow our minds."

Bowie is both the narrator and the protagonist of *Ziggy Stardust*, which tells the tale of how Ziggy comes to Earth, becomes a rock star, attempts to save humanity from itself, then flames out in a blaze of extraterrestrial glory. In its most basic form, the plot isn't that far from that of *Stranger in a Strange Land*, Robert Heinlein's 1961 novel about Valentine Michael Smith, a human raised on Mars who returns to Earth as an adult in an attempt to understand and be understood. And it feels like more than a coincidence that another science-fiction novel—Philip K. Dick's 1956 *The World Jones Made*—features hermaphroditic mutants who offer post-apocalyptic entertainment.

Bowie also loved *A Clockwork Orange*, both the film and the Anthony Burgess book on which it was based—and would later go on stage to the strains of Wendy Carlos's futuristic synthesizer score. One of *Ziggy Stardust*'s most popular songs, "Suffragette City," even cites the marauding "droogies" of *A Clockwork Orange*. The entire album is a web of disguises, smokescreens, allusions, delusions, mythic adventurism, and lavish decadence on par with any of Michael Moorcock's Jerry Cornelius stories.

Bowie's next incarnation, the short-lived, Ziggy-esque Aladdin Sane, was an anti-hero of his 1973 album of the same name. Less conceptual than *Ziggy Stardust*, *Aladdin Sane* features one solidly science-fictional song, "Drive-In Saturday." Despite the nostalgic sound, which draws heavily from '50s doo-wop, it takes place in the year 2033, when post-apocalyptic Earthlings are urged by "the strange ones in the domes" to reproduce, aided by the viewing of 20th-century pornography. At first it seems like an avant-pulp idea straight from the head of Burroughs, who

in a now-classic 1974 *Rolling Stone* interview, described Bowie's London home as being "decorated in a science-fiction mode."

Primarily, though, "Drive-In Saturday" resembles Kurt Vonnegut's satirical sci-fi novel from 1969, *Slaughterhouse-Five*. In it, protagonist Billy Pilgrim is placed in an extraterrestrial zoo—shaped like a dome, no less—and paired with a porn star in order for them to procreate. It's as though Bowie catapulted himself far beyond the sexual liberation hedonism of early-'70s rock culture and into some far stranger sexual tomorrow.

As if to punctuate that arc, Bowie's 1974 album *Diamond Dogs* is graced with cover art that depicts him in the midst of another "wild mutation," from a human being into a canine. It's his most sci-fi-heavy album, and his bleakest. Based on George Orwell's *1984* (Orwell's widow, Sonia Orwell, denied Bowie permission to do an official musical adaptation of the iconic novel, to Bowie's frustration), *Diamond Dogs* retains direct Orwell references in the song titles "We Are the Dead" and "Big Brother." According to a press release, *Diamond Dogs* "conceptualizes the vision of a future world with images of urban decadence and collapse," a mood that was also gripping sci-fi at the time, in films like *Soylent Green* and *A Boy and His Dog* and in the novels *334* by Thomas M. Disch and *Dhalgren* by Samuel R. Delany. And indeed, *Diamond Dogs*' opening track, "Future Legend," describes a scene of rotting corpses and "red mutant eyes" that could have been ripped straight from any of those harrowing, hopelessly grim works.

Bowie would return to speculative themes sporadically in subsequent years. But with glam still big business in the mid-'70s (and science fiction about to conquer popular culture thanks to *Star Wars*), other artists swooped in to fill his cosmic vacuum—most famously Elton John with his 1972 hit "Rocket Man," which was so similar to Bowie's works that rock critic Lester Bangs jestingly lumped them together, writing in *Creem* that Bowie looked as if he had been "dipped in vats of green slime and pursued by Venusian crab boys."

Two of the other most notable sci-fi-leaning musicians of the '70s were also Bowie collaborators: Marc Bolan of T. Rex and Brian Eno of Roxy Music. Bolan's space-age boogie merged Tolkienesque fantasy with the pulp sci-fi of Edgar Rice Burroughs's John Carter of Mars. Bolan and Bowie shared a producer, Tony Visconti, and the two had known each other since they played the same British club circuit in the '60s, venues with

sci-fi and fantasy-themed names such as the UFO Club and Middle Earth. Bolan also provided backing vocals on "Memory of a Free Festival," and at one point in the summer of 1974, Bowie and Bolan spent days bingeing on a print of *A Clockwork Orange*, a testament to just how much the science fiction of Kubrick and Burgess affected them.

As for Eno, his 1977 album *Before and After Science* hinted at the more rarified New Wave voices of Moorcock with lyrics such as "We're sailing at the edges of time," from "Backwater." And in 1979, Eno recorded the background music for an audio recording of Robert Sheckley's sci-fi novella *In a Land of Clear Colours*. By the end of the '70s, Eno had left glam far behind, focusing instead on ambient music. In 1983 he released *Apollo: Atmosphere and Soundtracks*, which accompanied a documentary that focused on the same NASA moon program that inspired Bowie a decade and a half before, bringing glam's interplay between science fact and science fiction full circle.

Eno's connection to Bowie runs deeper than the incidental bookends of "Space Oddity" and *Apollo*. Bowie's Berlin Trilogy—comprising 1977's *Low* and *"Heroes"* plus *Lodger* from 1979—were collaborations with Eno that resulted in some of the most challenging and innovative music of their respective careers. Oddly, though, it's one of the least sci-fi-leaning periods in Bowie's catalog—at least when it comes to lyrical matters. Sonically, Eno and Bowie crafted a sleek, automaton-like form of pop music on the Berlin Trilogy that seemed as eerily futurist as any Philip K. Dick novel (or any record by Kraftwerk, the German electronic band that Eno and Bowie found so fascinating at the time). That sound would vastly influence a new musical movement waiting just on the horizon: new wave.

The fact that Bowie, by the late '70s, served as the bridge between the sci-fi-heavy music genre of new wave and the sci-fi literary genre of New Wave is telling—especially as Bowie himself was about to complete a different kind of circuit. On his 1980 album *Scary Monsters (and Super Creeps)*, he included a song titled "Ashes to Ashes"; in it, an astronaut has become "strung out in heaven's high." The astronaut is Major Tom, and Bowie points out the link in the song's opening verse by breaking the fourth wall and directly addressing the listener: "Do you remember a guy that's been / In such an early song / I've heard a rumor from Ground Control / Oh no, don't say it's true."

"Ashes to Ashes" is a sequel to "Space Oddity," but it also stands as a testament to

Bowie's attachment to science fiction and fantasy. In *The Complete David Bowie*, Nicholas Pegg points out that Bowie's 1987 song "Girls" paraphrases a line from one of the singer's favorite sci-fi movies—Ridley Scott's *Blade Runner*, based on Dick's 1968 novel *Do Androids Dream of Electric Sheep?* That film's premise of androids who lose the ability to realize they're not human couldn't be more Bowie-esque. (Or vice versa.)

Major Tom would resurface again in "Hallo Spaceboy" from Bowie's 1995 album *Outside*, which found him reuniting with Eno for the first time in 15 years. Detailing a dystopian society on the verge of the new millennium, the album is a bleak work, one that Bowie claims to have "strong smatterings of *Diamond Dogs*." *Outside*'s follow-up, 1997's *Earthling*, retained a vestige of that sci-fi atmosphere, only with a more celestial slant.

In 2013, following nearly a decade of silence, Bowie released *The Next Day*, whose themes of mortality and outer space called back to Ziggy Stardust. In June of that year, Bowie was inducted into the Science Fiction and Fantasy Hall of Fame, the first musician to be awarded that honor. Near the end of 2013, he listed his top 100 books of all time, showcasing a broad literary panorama that spotlighted speculative-fiction classics such as Mikhail Bulgakov's *The Master and Margarita* and Angela Carter's *Nights at the Circus* alongside *1984* and *A Clockwork Orange* (not to mention Junot Díaz's *The Brief Wondrous Life of Oscar Wao*, whose main character, a boy infatuated with science fiction and fantasy novels, might have seemed familiar to someone who grew up reading Heinlein's *Starman Jones*).

"Around this time, Bowie's link with outer space and science fiction was consummated in a more profound way—one he never could have foreseen as a child in postwar London. On May 12, 2013, Canadian astronaut Chris Hadfield posted a YouTube video that featured him singing and playing an acoustic version of "Space Oddity" while in orbit on the International Space Station. It soon went viral, racking up more than 30 million views. And with it, mythology became fact, and a postmodern narrative went into the even stranger realm of the real.

The most staggering moment on Bowie's swansong, *Blackstar*, appears in the science-fiction video for its 10-minute title track. An unknown planet—or perhaps it's our planet, far in the future or past—orbits an ominous sun that's either become eclipsed or burns with some perpetual darkness. A girl with a tail, straight out of a fantasy novel, finds a

figure in a NASA-style space suit reclining against a rock. As if answering the helmet-donning gesture of Major Tom in the video for "Space Oddity" 46 years earlier, the astronaut's visor is raised. Behind it is a skull encrusted with jewels and gold filigree, the ornamented corpse of a space traveler left to spin through eternity. □

HIS BARK AND HIS BITE

▸ *continued from page 69*

there is no pattern there, that it's just one endless miasmic experience. And that's when it really gets very serious because then you have to start contemplating that there may be a situation where there is no God, and that for me would be ultimately disheartening.

The older you get, do you become closer to God?
Less and less. That's what I'm finding.

Isn't that the wrong thing to do, though?
Graham Greene would say so. I don't know what Samuel Beckett would have said. I mean, I never really understood what he thought at the end. All I know is that his last words were: "What a morning" [*actually, the last words of his father, Bill Beckett*]. I just think, "Oh God, I hope I can come up with something like that: 'Oh, what a morning!'" When I had a stronger link with Buddhism, it was easy for me to think that there was a force rather than a God, and not to adopt a position on God; so it's not such an odd position for me to want to come to—but it sort of negates any spiritual life.

Well, if we accept mortality— which we must—it is not like you haven't left your mark on the world. But does the success of something like *Heathen* change your ambition and make you think, "Well, I've got 15 good years left

in me, or 20 or 25, and what am I going to fill them with?"
But that's the thing. I wonder if it's worth filling them; I'm not so sure that there is any purpose, and that's the thing that really starts to confound me. I don't do it with a sinking sense of negativity; I can actually feel quite content with the idea that nothing's important.

How does it change your ambition?
Ambition, there's a thing. Ambition is kind of a series of expectations, so yes it's certainly mellowed it. I am enjoying working in the present. I am enjoying day-to-day existence much more than I ever did before. You know, maybe I'm just collecting all this survivalist armory of philosophical ideas that will shore up the idea that we should live in the now. We are just a species dependent on survival instincts, and that's how we build up our moralities, absolutes, and truths. Good and evil we have created ourselves because those two things help us survive as a unity and as a species. There is no basis that one is superior to the other. And I think a lot of evil is just a series of dysfunctions.

Were you in New York City on September 11, or were you in the studio recording?
I personally wasn't—I was up north, in Woodstock, in the album mines. Iman was there with our baby so, of course, psychologically it was unbelievably traumatic because I wasn't on the bloody spot. And it was all done by phone, until the phones were cut off. Oh man, I can't tell you how scary that was. That was terrifying. 'Cause the thing happened and I was talking to Iman, and she was saying, "Oh my God, a second one has gone in." Boom! And I said, "Get the fuck out of there: You're under attack." It was so obvious to me, as soon as the second one hit. It was like, Jesus Christ, they're being attacked. I said, "Get the pram, and just put all the essentials in it and get the hell out of there." She rushed up about 15, 20 blocks, just literally running with the pram, and then got to her friend's, because we're quite a way downtown. I said, "Call me when you get to a place of safety," and of course she never called back because all the lines were down. I thought, "No, no, not now. Did she get out?" And of course nobody knew anything. And then all the roads got cut off. We couldn't drive into New York because the police had the city surrounded. You couldn't get in, couldn't get out. It was really awful.

I went in January and the city was dead. There was a palpable change. It ain't dead now—although there's kind of a slight caution behind the eyes of all New Yorkers now, a little tension behind the eyes that I hadn't seen before. Well, it's probably something they could use in a way. They've been so protected, so innocent of the realities of an international situation. It's like everybody else has kind of had a bit of it, and now unfortunately for the Americans it's their turn.

Are you surprised that there have been so few relevant cultural responses to September 11?
People don't have a clear idea of what they believe to be right and wrong anymore. I think people are frankly numbed. Not many people are so certain about what it is that they think, and they're not quite so quick to jump to the defense of one side or the other. It's such confusion, nobody knows anything anymore. You know, it's a fast-receding past, an incredibly uncertain future, and a diminishing present. There's a great blurring of everything in our lives now. It's far more about how me and my family are going to get through the day.

You must love the anonymity of living in New York.
It's great. The sense of humor is quite difficult, though. What's the time, or should I go fuck myself now? You know, they're tough people.

Have your experiences with your daughter, Lexi, encouraged you to have more children?
I don't think so; I think I'm too old. Unless we adopt—and we have talked about that. But we would adopt a child who is already a few years in. You know, I can really concentrate on what Lexi wants and help her make choices. I don't know, I'm very happy with just one. It'd be very nice for her to have a younger brother when she is about three or four, but I think we would adopt then.

What happened to the Ziggy project?
I did sit down with a couple of guys about two or three years ago. We endeavored to put a shape to it as a theatrical piece and it was a nonstarter. The more I wrote into it, the smaller and smaller it just seemed to be. And one of the guys actually posed the question, "Why are you doing this?" He said it means a lot to people—didn't I feel that by developing him, I would be closing

up all the possibilities to the character? He said if I devised a formidable storyline, I'd probably be ruining everybody's ideas. We kind of got to the consensus that we would probably be doing the whole idea of Ziggy a disservice by nailing it. I think its major strength is that there was such an ephemeral quality to the whole business, and it left so many options open for people to read into themselves. That was his valuable service to humanity: I'm Ziggy, use me.

You were the first artist to initiate a bond issue against future royalties ["Bowie Bonds" raised £38 million—$55 million—in 1997, with past albums as collateral]. How successful was it?
Extremely. It was very solvent. My business partner came up with the idea and we both wondered why nobody had ever done it before. A few people have been able to do it, but the major obstacle in doing anything like that is that you've got to own your stuff, otherwise it's not going to work. A lot of writers have given away or have lost control of their publishing, and you have to own your publishing to be able to do it.

What's the best thing about traveling on the QE2?
Well, right now, at this moment, I've got my phobia about flying back again. I'm coping with it to a certain extent. I flew the whole of Europe. We flew. But I just can't face that transatlantic trip. I don't want to be on a plane going over the Atlantic. I got my phobia before September 11—it started when my baby was born.

What's it like being on the ship, though? Is it fun?
Oh, I love it. It's like this hotel, only at sea. But bigger. I mean, you cannot believe how big the *Queen Elizabeth* is. It's bigger than this hotel. It's got five restaurants, two cinemas, two or three theaters. Gymnasiums. Swimming pools. Shopping malls. I mean, it's just beyond... There's about 1,800 passengers. But there's also about 1,800 crew to look after you. I've never been on a Caribbean cruise but I get the impression that it's a bit Club Med and a lot of party nights, and all that stuff. But the QE2 isn't like that. People who go across the Atlantic go for very different reasons. I think a lot of people bring books with them, and they're quieter, more academic. I've bumped into writers, musicians, painters, politicians, and, on the last trip, John

Cleese. I wanted to see what it was like to be adrift for seven days. It's a challenge, because you know you're not going to stop off at any exotic locations.

And so a normal day for you on the QE2 would consist of what exactly?
I sleep in and try to get up at around seven. Then I order a quick breakfast or muesli or porridge, or whatever. Then I normally go and jog round the deck, which is like a fifth of a mile, and so you do a few rounds of that. Then I do some regular aerobic lifting. And then in the afternoon I'll just lounge around reading. I usually take an enormous number of books with me. I'm quite happy... I can read all day long and float between two or three books at the same time. And then I go down and choose which restaurant I'm going to have lunch in. I tend to ask for solo sitting, because I can take a book with me for lunch. But then at dinner I usually see who else is around on board, and who's on my table, and kind of stick with it.

And do you write?
Yeah, absolutely. I initially start my ideas in longhand and then go to the computer and work in Word. What I always tend to do as well is take DVDs with me on those trips. I take a lot of stuff that possibly my family doesn't particularly get on too well with. I take, like, really long Russian films and things like that. Something by Andrei Tarkovsky or Krzysztof Kieslowski.

What are you reading at the moment?
I'm reading Martin Amis's *The War Against Cliché*—it's great because you can dip in and out of it. But you have to have a dictionary with you when you read Amis because on every page—guaranteed—there's going to be one word where you think, "What the fuck is that?" And, of course, a regular little dictionary doesn't have it all. I have to keep going online to get one of the big dictionaries. He's pulling up words that you've never seen before.

What's your waist size?
Thirty.

Can a person ever be too thin?
I've never really thought about that. Well, I certainly was. I have various photographs of me looking skeletal, which remind me how badly behaved I was back in the '70s. They're Polaroids as well, which makes it even worse because they're badly lit. I occasionally look at them and think, "How did I ever get to

that state? How did I survive it?" Yeah, you can be too thin!

You've been through so many reincarnations and had so many public images—I think that the only thing you could actually do that you haven't done is to get fat.
The fat Bowie. Well, maybe when I move into the Las Vegas circuit...

What was your best-ever look?
You see, the thing is, you know what I'm like. I'm not that interested in fashion, as long as I'm comfortable. But I do know the importance of how a way of looking denotes your attitude to whatever it is you're supposed to be involved with. So for me, dressing is performance. I must be honest. I'm very comfortable about what's happening with me at the moment. There's enough theatricality to the clothes that I'm now using on stage... I'm working with Hedi Slimane, who I love, and Lee [Alexander McQueen], who also does stuff for me. I think both those guys are just tremendous designers.

Ironically, you've always said you hated fashion. What was your worst look?
I always looked O.K. in clothes—I was kind of a target for designers, always. They sort of made a beeline for me and tried to get me to wear these things. But I guess it was up to me to choose which ones I would wear. Sometimes I was right, sometimes I wasn't. I should never have touched the Culture Shock label in the early '80s.

What's the worst thing you've ever put in your mouth?
I was in Hong Kong on holiday with John Lennon in the late '70s. We'd been drinking and we were trying to find a place to eat monkeys' brains. We actually found a place, but fortunately it was closed. However, we saw the tables, and I think it was at that point that we both decided that we weren't going to come back: We saw the tables with the holes in them—they put the monkey through the hole, whip its skull off and eat it like an egg. But we both lingered and a couple of guys recognized Lennon. They took him in a back room, and he came out and said, "God, I'm as high as a kite." They'd made him drink the blood of a snake. I guess it was a Triad thing, but it made him very stoned.

Anyway, he went off and then came rushing down the road a few minutes later,

saying, "Open your mouth!" And he shoved this thing in my mouth—it was ghastly. I asked him what it was and he said, "Swallow it." So I did. And he said, "That's a thousand-day-old egg cooked in horse piss!" I said, "You bastard!" They cook it in horse urine, then cover it in layers of different kinds of manures and bury it into the ground. I think they probably bury it only for a few days, but they call it a thousand-day-old egg. They dig it up again and then you eat it. It was horrible.

Most people think that Lennon was trapped in America during that time.
No, what he used to do was carry a briefcase with just his wallet and a T-shirt in it, and he used to travel like that all the time. When he got to a new place and his T-shirt needed washing, he'd give it to the waiter or the bellboy. He'd sign it for them and then buy another one off the street. He'd get everything else from the hotel—a razor or whatever he needed. He would say, "That's how you travel." Of course it makes sense, but I haven't got the bottle [courage] to do that.

I suppose the period when he was going abroad a bit was when he had that strange thing going, when he wasn't really with Yoko. But his son Sean was with him. He took a nanny with him as well, but John was with Sean an awful lot in Hong Kong—except we used to go out at night and get raving drunk.

One night we ended up at a strip club where beers were served at a round table, with a naked girl sitting in the middle of it and spinning around slowly. John was getting quite verbose because he had really put away quite a few, and the owner of the club asked us to leave. So we were thrown out by these, presumably, lesser Triad members. We're on the sidewalk, and John is frothing at the mouth and shouting, "Let us back in! We've paid our money, we want to come in and finish our drinks!" And they said, "No, you fuck off." And he said, "Do you know who I am? I'm a fucking Beatle!" I said, "I don't believe that. Say it again." He said, "I'm a fucking Beatle, I'm a fucking Beatle!" and we started laughing. We were just on the floor, it was so funny. And then we went to a street market and they were selling Beatle jackets, and I got him to put one on. I took a little Polaroid; I've still got it, it's so lovely. Just John and his Beatle jacket. "I'm a fucking Beatle!" □

10 BEST ALBUMS

▸ *continued from page 95*
will connect me with love?" To fans who don't hate the pair of six-minute ballads, this is a masterpiece. **Don't overlook:** "Stay"

LOW *(1977)*
Bowie fled the cocaine hills of L.A. and moved to Europe, then made an album with "oodles of pain," he later said. There's also humor ("You're such a wonderful person, but you've got problems" is one of his best bon mots) amid the clipped electronic pop and stately instrumentals. Though he sounds fazed and dazed, *Low* is his cleverest album. **Don't overlook:** "Be My Wife"

"HEROES" *(1977)*
"It's louder and harder" than its predecessor, *Low*, Bowie said, and also "far more psychotic." Aside from several chilly instrumentals, the big exception to the album's tense, piercing mood is the title song, a rare instance of Bowie evoking specific emotions: struggle, hope, maybe even triumph. **Don't overlook:** "V-2 Schneider"

SCARY MONSTERS (AND SUPER CREEPS) *(1980)*
New wave stole a lot from Bowie—his wardrobe, his makeup, his svelte glamour—and here he grabs it back, with a collection of disturbed, uncanny dance songs. In "Ashes to Ashes," he all but burns the costumes of his '70s photo shoots by depicting old friend Major Tom as a psychotic drug addict, symbolically ending the epic second phase of Bowie's career. **Don't overlook:** "Teenage Wildlife"

LET'S DANCE *(1983)*
Among Bowie's many guises, this was the strangest: global pop superstar. With help from producer Nile Rodgers, the singer transformed himself from an oddball with occasional chart success into a revered rock elder. He made a few more pop albums, then had an epiphany ("I sound like Phil Collins") and returned to abrasive rock'n'roll. **Don't overlook:** "Criminal World"

BLACKSTAR *(2016)*

He'd made only one album in the previous 12 years. Maybe he'd retired. Then, on his 69th birthday, he sent one last message: a record made at the unmapped intersection of rock, funk, and jazz. *Blackstar* is restless and evasive; full of puzzles, possible clues, and images of death. His vocals are faint. Was it weakness from the cancer that killed him? "Look up here, I'm in heaven," he sang. But really, he's all around us, too. **Don't over-look:** "I Can't Give Everything Away" □

A MAN OF THE MOVIES

▸ *continued from page 89*

man through the movies, offers double the value. It first appeared in Paul Schrader's *Cat People* (1982), and then emerged from the darkness once more, in 2009, when Quentin Tarantino unleashed it for *Inglourious Basterds.* (Bowie himself appears in neither film.) For that movie, as you would presume, the mood is utterly ensnared in cinematic references, with Shosanna Dreyfus (Mélanie Laurent) preparing herself for vengeance against an auditorium stuffed with Nazis, including Hitler and Goebbels. The physical flammability of film itself is deployed as a weapon, neatly bringing Bowie's conceit—"I've been putting out fire with gasoline"—to fruition. If there is a slight want of potency here, it is not Bowie's fault, but that of Giorgio Moroder, who is responsible for the music; like so many pulsing compositions of the '80s, it is littered with hooks but twistless, lacking that leap with which Bowie, left to his own devices and desires, would take care to supply.

No such meagerness attended *The Life Aquatic with Steve Zissou* (2004), which permitted Wes Anderson to pour forth his devotion to Bowie. Being Anderson, he insured that the pouring was largely done at an oblique angle, thanks to Seu Jorge, who performed well-known Bowie numbers in Portuguese, as though insisting that we could and should know them anew. His

rendition of "Starman" is at once brisk and relaxed, and shot without adornment, by night; he tucks his half-smoked cigarette into the head of his acoustic guitar, next to the tuning pegs, sings, finishes, retrieves his smoke, takes a puff, tosses the butt over his shoulder, exhales in a luminous billow, and receives a bout of applause. The sequence is as casual, and somehow as necessary, as Feste's pausing the folderol of *Twelfth Night* to grace us with "Come Away, Death" and his other songs—jester's riffs, of no consequence, except that their swift meditations on mortality and love will linger in the mind's ear long after the play is done.

Not to be left out, Bill Murray, too, in the title role, takes a deep draught of Bowie. One evening, aboard his ship, he is so whelmed by emotion, as he talks to the fellow he believes to be his son (Owen Wilson), that his only option is to shake hands and say, "I'll be right back. Don't go away." He then sets off along the boat, the camera tracking his progress, and, as he does so, the soundtrack explodes—"Sailors, fighting in the dance hall…" This is not Jorge's Bowie, lovely though it is, but the man himself, at his most ecstatic, in the chorus from "Life on Mars?," and, as Zissou stands in the prow, perfectly calm and composed in his regulation tuxedo and red knit hat, we realize that Anderson is doing what millions of others have done before: He is handing over his feelings to David Bowie, and letting a song do all the work of the heart. Why write dialogue when the wild exclamations of another artist, recorded in 1971, will give vent to everything that you want your characters to say—or, rather, what they cannot say because it is all too much? Such is the yearning that beats throughout this scene. You can see it 10 times or more. It is never a saddening bore.

That, more or less, is what Bowie means to the movies. Once you start hunting for it, you stumble across it without warning, in the nooks of unlikely films. "I should go," Greta Gerwig says to Adam Driver in *Frances Ha* (2012). She's over at his place. He says, "Before you go, do us another dance," and she, being Frances, complies, jumping up and down as if clinging to an unseen pogo stick. That seems to meet the case, but she has more to express, and so it is that we cut to an external shot, and to the opening bars of Bowie's "Modern Love." Our heroine is running now, allying herself with the cause of all those figures who, for whatever reason, have capered or sprinted through New York—Shirley MacLaine at the end of *The Apartment,* Dustin Hoffman in *Kramer*

vs. Kramer, and Woody Allen in *Manhattan,* racing to refind the girl he should never have let go. Gerwig, in leggings, sneakers, and a floral dress, adds a few long prances of her own, like somebody crossing a stream, and spins around for the hell of it, or for the bliss of hearing Bowie in her head. Then, back at her apartment, she shuts the door, and instantly the music stops. Love is most modern, it would seem, not in the cloistered cells of our homes, but out on the street.

And so to 14th-century England—an obvious shift, since Bowie is banned from no location. At a formal banquet, the nefarious host demands that his guest from afar, Sir Ulrich, demonstrate a dance from his own land. Briefly confounded, Sir Ulrich recovers and begins to move. A lute twangs, a fife pipes up, fiddles do their thing, and the revelers clap their hands. Gradually, the tempo increases, the lonely word "Angel" descends from on high, and at some imperceptible juncture, we find ourselves in Bowie's "Golden Years," with the assembled company, in their silks and snoods, squaring up to boogie. This passage—the highlight of Brian Helgeland's *A Knight's Tale* (2001), with Heath Ledger—is the best and most honest use of anachronism that I know of. It summons the gold of our own years and sends it back in time to gild another age. Rather than saddle us with some cod-medieval lumbering, the movie comes clean, as if to say: We don't know what these folk listened to, and it wouldn't mean much to us if we did, but we can guess that they were inspired enough to dance, and we know what inspiration sounds like. It sounds like Bowie.

And so, with his death, the dance is over, though not quite. His final album, *Blackstar,* came out the week of his death, and the video of one song, "Lazarus," finds Bowie not only in bed, with a bandaged face, reporting on his current situation—"Look up here, I'm in heaven"—but upright and poised, as if for one last jive, in his last ever catsuit. He shudders and takes a backward pace, and then another, in a kind of wounded moonwalk: Major Tom, floating in a most peculiar way, reversing into a wardrobe and closing the door. "Knowledge comes with death's release," he sang in "Quicksand"—the closing track on the unimprovable Side One of *Hunky Dory,* and the most sumptuous of his many choruses. What David Bowie knows now, and what Narnia awaits him in the wardrobe, none can tell. But his life, unlike most lives, had the shape and the refulgence of a movie, and we can watch it again and again. □

THE BRILLIANCE OF DAVID BOWIE

CONTENT DEVELOPMENT GROUP

Creative Director
RAÚL MARTINEZ

Director, Special Interest Publishing
LEAH McLAUGHLIN

Design Director
ANDRZEJ JANERKA

Editor
TOM PRINCE

Managing Editor
GREG FERRO

Deputy Editor
DOUG BROD

Art Directors
KAREN HIBBERT,
EFFENDY WIJAYA

Senior Editors
CATHY CAVENDER,
FAN WINSTON

Designer
HSIAO-PIN LIN

Photo Director
MARIANNE BUTLER

Photo Editor
MARK JACOBSON

Associate Editors
ANTONINA JEDRZEJCZAK, MICHAEL THOMSEN

Production
KEIGHT BERGMANN, KELLEY ERICKSON,
JIM SCHUESSLER, DIANE WILLIAMS

Photo Researcher
OMOTOMI OMOLOLU-LANGE

Copy
KATIE KRETSCHMER

Research
TIMOTHY HODLER, JOYCE PENDOLA

Editorial Assistants
ANGELICA FREY, ISAAC LOBEL, REBECCA PATTON

Executive Director, Special Projects
CHRISTIANE MACK

Artistic Director
ANNA WINTOUR

CREDITS

FRONT COVER
Herb Ritts/Trunk Archive.

CONTENTS
Inside cover: © Mick Rock.

REBEL REBEL
2: Terry O'Neill/Getty Images.
4: Terry O'Neill/Getty Images.
6: *Clockwise from left:* Courtesy of David Bowie/Distributed Art Publisher; Photograph by Roy Ainsworth/ Courtesy of The David Bowie Archive 2012/Image © V&A Images; © Retna Pictures/Photoshot; © Pictorial Press Ltd/Alamy Stock Photo.
7: © Daily Mirror/Mirrorpix/Corbis.
8: © Masayoshi Sukita/Courtesy of Morrison Hotel Gallery.
9: © Duffy Archive & The David Bowie Archive ™.
10-11: *From left:* Terry O'Neill/Getty Images; © Steve Schapiro/Corbis; Ron Galella/Getty images; GAB Archive/ Getty Images (Crosby); SNL/NBC. (SNL); © RTNWhite/MediaPunch; GAB Archive/Getty Images; ALP/ MediaPunch (Live Aid).
12: *Clockwise from top left:* Camera Press/ Brian Aris/Redux; Miramax/Courtesy Neal Peters Collection; Andrew McCafferty/REX Shutterstock; © Pictorial Press Ltd/Alamy Stock Photo (Tin Machine).
13: *Clockwise from top left:* KMazur/ Getty Images; © Jimmy King; © dpa picture alliance/Alamy Stock Photo (Lazarus).

STARMAN
14: © Mick Rock/courtesy Taschen.
17: © Mick Rock.
18: *From top:* © First Look Pictures/ Everett Collection; Leee Black Childers/Getty Images.
19: *From top:* © Mick Rock; Roberta Bayley/Getty Images; Ann Limongello/Getty Images.
20-21: Ilpo Musto/REX Shutterstock.
23: David Bebbington/© Retna/ Photoshot.
24: NASA/REX Shutterstock (Hadfield).
25: *Clockwise from top left:* RCA Records (Ashes to Ashes); © Photos 12/Alamy Stock Photo (Clockwork Orange); Kevin Bray/MGM/Photofest.
26: Andy Kent/© LFI/Photoshot.
27: *Clockwise from left:* © LFI/Photoshot; Dave Hogan/Getty Images; © Mick Rock.
28: *Clockwise from top left:* Ron Galella/ Getty Images; Ebet Roberts/Getty Images; © Mick Rock; Denis O'Regan/ Getty Images (Jagger).
29: Photograph by Terry O'Neill. Hand colouring by David Bowie. Courtesy of The David Bowie Archive 2012. Image © V&A Images.
30-31: Terry O'Neill/Getty Images.
32-33: © Steve Schapiro/Corbis.
35: *From top:* © dpa picture alliance/ Alamy Stock Photo.

FASHION
36: © Mick Rock/courtesy Taschen.
40: © Michael Kim/Corbis.
41: Debi Doss/Getty Images.
42-43: Snowdon/Trunk Archive.
44: Chris Foster/REX Shutterstock.
45: Mert Alas & Marcus Piggott/Trunk Archive.
46: Sebastian Kim/ Management+Artists.
47: Craig McDean/Art+Commerce.
48-49: Nick Knight/Trunk Archive.
50: David Sims/Trunk Archive.
51: Tim Walker/CLM.
52-53: Craig McDean/Art+Commerce.
54-55: Kim Weston Arnold (Margiela); Yannis Vlamos (Dior; Gaultier); Chris Moore/Catwalking/Getty Images (Lanvin; Pam Hogg); Giovanni Giannoni (Givenchy; Saint Laurent; Dries; Balmain).

GOLDEN YEARS
57: Camera Press/Brian Aris/Redux.
63: Greg Gorman/Getty Images.
65: Rankin/Trunk Archive.
70-71: © Barry Schultz/Sunshine/ ZUMA.
72: Patrick Jarnoux/Getty Images.

SOUND AND VISION
81-83: Mario Testino/Art Partner.
85: Everett Collection.
86: From top: © AF archive/Alamy Stock Photo; © United Artist/Courtesy Everett Collection.
87: © Miramax/Photofest.
88-89: *Clockwise from top left:* Cinema 5/ Courtesy Neal Peters Collection; © Universal/Courtesy Everett Collection; © Orion/Courtesy Everett Collection; TriStar Pictures/Courtesy Neal Peters Collection (Labyrinth).
90-91: Camera Press/Clive Arrowsmith/Redux.
92: © Mick Rock.
93: Columbia Records.
94: © Christian Simonpietri/Sygma/ Corbis.
96-97: Courtesy of Columbia Records.

ASHES TO ASHES
99: Snowdon/Trunk Archive.
100: Jorgen Angel/Getty Images.
112 and inside back cover: Camera Press/Carolyn Djanogly/Redux.

BACK COVER
© Mick Rock.

Some of the images in this special edition were shot by Mick Rock, whose upcoming book, *The Rise of David Bowie, 1972–1973* (Taschen, $69.99), chronicles the period in which he served as Bowie's official photographer and features many previously unpublished photos.

"I'M VERY GLAD THAT I GOT THIS LIFE. IT'S A GIFT."

OPEN AND SHUT
The artist in 1999.

**PHOTOGRAPHS BY
CAROLYN DJANOGLY**